New Architects 2
A guide to Britain's best young architectural practices

The Architecture Foundation

MERRELL

Published by Merrell Publishers Limited
42 Southwark Street
London SE1 1UN
www.merrellpublishers.com

First published 2001

Distributed in the USA and Canada by
Rizzoli International Publications, Inc. through
St Martin's Press, 175 Fifth Avenue, New York,
New York 10010

British Library Cataloguing-in-Publication Data:
New Architects2 : a guide to Britain's best young architectural practices
1.Architectural firms – Great Britain – Directories
2.Architecture, Modern – 20th century – Great Britain
I.Architecture Foundation
724.6'06041

ISBN 1 85894 138 5

Designed by
Esterson Lackersteen

Colour reproduction by Precise Litho

Compiled and edited by
Wordsearch Communications
5 Old Street
London EC1V 9HL

Printed and bound in Italy

Supported by
cabe

Sponsored by
DELANCEY
ESTATES LTD

New Architects 2

I am very pleased to have had the opportunity to sponsor *New Architects 2*, not least because as a young company ourselves, Delancey had first-hand experience of the obstacles that often stand in the way of new businesses as they evolve and establish their identity. Architects can find their artistic and design integrity compromised by the commercial world, which is driven by both the need for 'a safe pair of hands' and the 'bottom line'. Sacrificing design does not always lead to increased profit; quite the opposite can be true. A building of integrity and quality in which value is generated through good and compelling design can pay handsomely when presented to an ever-more-willing and accepting marketplace.

I very much hope that this book will be used and enjoyed by a wide audience, and that any projects arising from it will contribute positively to our national architectural heritage.

James Ritblat
Chairman
Delancey Estates

Contents

Preface
Tony Blair

The United Kingdom is full of young talent, contributing to the vibrancy of the creative industries which are a vital part of our economic success.

Architecture is an important part of this scene, but it is a discipline in which it can be difficult for newcomers to win recognition. So the Architecture Foundation's publication of *New Architects* in 1998 was an important landmark and I welcome this new edition. Here is a presentation not of established architects, but of young practices with some achievements and a lot of promise. These are the emerging practices from which some of the stars of the future will emerge.

I am committed to encouraging a new age of good design in our public buildings, so that we match the best of that which we have inherited from previous generations. I want to see a step change in the quality of what we build, particularly with the substantial increase in capital spending which we have already announced. But that does not necessarily mean commissioning big well-known architects for every project. As this book makes clear, there is a wealth of talent to be found in the new generation, and smaller practices may be particularly suitable for modest-sized jobs at a local level.

I commend The Architecture Foundation for providing this new showcase for the new generation of architects. I hope that clients in the public and private sectors will look in this book, see what has already been achieved by these young practices, and consider whether they can be given further opportunities.

Introduction
Sir Stuart Lipton

CABE was delighted to help in the production of this publication. While quality is always our primary concern, CABE is committed to promoting the work of new architectural practices across England in a way that reflects the strength of our cultural diversity.

CABE is the champion for architecture in England. Our function is to promote high standards in the design of buildings and the spaces between them. CABE's vision is to inject architecture into the bloodstream of the nation so that Britain becomes the European leader in prioritizing the quality of the built environment through both public and private investment.

CABE's aims, amongst others, are to foster public awareness and appreciation of good design in architecture and the built environment and encourage public involvement in its creation, and to promote better design for the cultural, social and economic and environmental benefits it brings to society. Our work is based on core values that include increasing the diversity of the construction industry in terms of ethnicity, gender, disability and age profile. This will increase the skills base and improve the quality of buildings and places. We are for architecture, not architects. While the skills of a good architect are fundamental and irreplaceable in ensuring a high quality product, the architect is only one player in the team that will ensure the right end result.

This publication addresses many of our core aims and objectives and will prove an invaluable tool for the procurement of architects. In improving and enlightening clients, in both the public and private sectors, the burgeoning talents of the practices in this directory will be harnessed and encouraged.

CABE works in partnership with many people and organisations – such as the National Architecture Centre Network, of which the Architecture Foundation is a member. The Foundation has produced an excellent book and key resource that will advocate the current best young practices to a wider audience.

Sir Stuart Lipton, Chairman
Commission for Architecture
and the Built Environment (CABE)

Foreword
Richard Rogers
Will Alsop

This is the second publication in the *New Architects* series that highlights the Architecture Foundation's ongoing commitment to celebrating the work of new and emerging British practices. In doing so, it aims to promote high-quality contemporary architecture and urban design to as wide an audience as possible.

Since the first publication in 1998, we have witnessed an explosion of Lottery-funded projects across the country. Caruso St John, included in the first *New Architects* publication, won the competition for Walsall's New Art Gallery, a Lottery-funded project totalling £21m. A major success on their part, it was, however, the only major Lottery building to open in 2000 that was designed by a young practice. If clients are commissioning large new-build projects, very few are choosing young and emerging practices, which suggests that there is little confidence or belief in them.

However, young British practices are in the habit of winning major commissions abroad, including, most recently, the £150m Yokohama Liner Terminal in Japan by Foreign Office Architects, or Sauerbruch Hutton's GSW office building in Berlin, Germany. Both are examples of significant commissions being given to emerging practices outside of the UK, which would indicate that juries and clients in this country either lack the courage to choose emerging practices, or that they are simply unaware of them. It is for this reason that *New Architects 2* will become a very useful guide.

From our experience, clients in this country are more likely to commission practices based solely on a track record of project-type. Yet, when a client is willing to take the risk, the collaboration is unexpected and extremely satisfying. Alsop Architects was given its first break when Blackfriars Investments Ltd, London, commissioned the practice to build its South Point office. Similarly, the turning point for Richard Rogers Partnership was the new-build for Reliance Controls Electronics Factory in Swindon, Wiltshire.

In this publication, we do not define 'young' by the age of the architect, but by the fact that we believe each practice selected has yet to be given the opportunity to build significant projects, and the benefits of commissioning young practices are manifold. Given a reasonable-sized project, a practice can be propelled from obscurity into a sustainable organisation. Another benefit, especially for the client, is being able to work closely with the practice partner for the duration of the project; a unique and creative experience in itself.

Delancey Estates, sponsors of this publication, invited virtually unknown practices to take part in a competition to contribute to their Parkfield Street, Islington scheme in north London. Their commission, for a kiosk and piece of street art, was purposely designed to attract submissions from those entrants ratified for *New Architects 2*, believing emerging practices to have as much skill, vision and tenacity as the big players. Through this exercise, not only does the client give young practices the chance to present their ideas, more importantly, architects bring new concepts and suggestions to the table beyond the initial call of the commission.

If, by producing the *New Architects* series, we have succeeded in bringing together one private-sector client with one emerging practice, then we have succeeded in promoting further high-quality contemporary architecture. This guide, therefore, is a continuation of that belief and, as in the first edition, we continually urge clients to integrate its use into their commissioning process. In addition, we hope this publication provides all readers with an understanding and appreciation of the next generation of British architectural practices.

**Richard Rogers, Founding Chair
and Will Alsop, Chair of
The Architecture Foundation**

Looking for the
next generation
Deyan Sudjic

There is a continuing and apparently powerful, if somewhat perverse, urge to write architecture off as dead. In fact the evidence points rather to the contrary. Charles Jencks, the critic who defined Post-modernism, a style that must itself be just on the edge of an irony-soaked rediscovery, used to confine himself to proclaiming the demise of Modernism. It was an event that he claimed to have detected in the dynamiting of that famous block of award-winning but unloved social housing, the Pruitt Igoe development in St Louis, America, back in the 1970s. The fact that so many architects carried on as if nothing had happened afterwards – "like so many headless chickens", as he put it – could be counted as one of the wonders of the age.

There are no such tortured defining moments for the newly emerging architectural voices in this book. They belong to a fortunate generation that began to practice at a time when the Bilbao Guggenheim in Spain, and the wave of Lottery-funded millennium projects in Britain, transformed the public appetite for architecture. These twenty and thirty-somethings started out working against the backdrop of a government with a relatively sophisticated approach to making architectural policy. You take it for granted as soon as it's there. But it wasn't always so easy.

Architecture can be like story telling. Each generation comes up with its own narratives that initially are treated like fairy tales. And then gradually, through constant repetition and the enormous seriousness with which the storytellers tell their tales, they turn from fiction into newspaper headlines. What else was the Pompidou Centre in Paris, France, in its day than a fantasy brought to life through sheer willpower? And what else is Lab Studio's Federation Square in Melbourne, Australia? Until you actually build an architectural complex in the form of a giant cultural machine, in the case of the Pompidou, or a geometrically ordered landscape, in the case of Federation Square, both propositions belong to the world of fantasy. But when an architect carries the conviction to turn the fantasy into physically reality, then the rules of the game change dramatically quickly. This is a generation that has come to maturity at a time when architecture is far from marginalized. It's a generation that manages to be bold, experimental, and one that is not afraid to make occasional mistakes.

Yet, in his more messianic moods, Rem Koolhaas,

perhaps the most celebrated graduate of the British architectural educational system in the last thirty years, is even more sweepingly bleak than Charles Jencks was. He does not hesitate to suggest that the practice of architecture, in all its forms, is defunct. Architecture as it was traditionally understood was, Koolhaas suggests, finally killed off by the invention of the escalator. It might have survived the lift, but architecture as a journey through a considered sequence of spaces, was killed by the moving staircase. Escalators, he suggests, accomplish the task of multiplying the value of a site far more effectively than architecture ever could. Escalators make the first floor of a building exactly the same as the ground floor or even the third floor. And so all the tricks and stratagems that architects have used for at least three thousand years to denote status and hierarchy became immediately redundant.

And yet, as the work published here demonstrates, architecture is clearly far from dead, even in the formal sense that Koolhaas implies. The more it seems that architecture is pronounced dead, the more it seems to flourish. It's a constantly inventive, constantly creative discipline, one that is blithely ready and willing, if not always able, to take on technology as well as philosophy, far beyond the level of its actual competencies. But that hardly matters when you are creating stories. It's ready to operate at the scale of the individual object as well as the megalopolis, to embrace the intensely physical as well as the immaterial.

Architecture can now be a wider range of things than it has ever been, ranging all the way from militant ecological activism to installation art. It's still possible for architects to aspire to the formal purity and detailed rigour of Mies van der Rohe, to use architecture to critique fashion, and vice versa. Architecture can be the route into urbanism or any amount of entrepreneurial development. It's about mud houses, and steel pods, salvaged sofas from the 1960s in fashionable bars, tributes to Buckminster Fuller and recalibrating conventional geometries. More to the point, none of these things need necessarily be mutually exclusive. Architecture now is being defined by architects who refuse to allow themselves to be isolated by strict ideological quarantines from other disciplines. Just look at the rather arch way that architectural practices now name themselves to sound like software operating systems, exotic vegetables, or parodies of Miesian bureaucracies. They don't want to rule themselves out

of anything that might come their way. Architecture is more fully part of a wider cultural landscape in Britain than at anytime since Reyner Banham, Richard Hamilton, Eduardo Paolozzi, the Smithsons and the young James Stirling first began to congregate in Soho, central London, on Saturday mornings in the early 1950s to talk about American pop-imagery, industrial design and the cult of the 'ready-made'. The students emerging from the British architecture schools in the last ten years, and their teachers who are now beginning to build on a large scale, take for granted the formal freedom, and the openness of clients to fresh thinking. And they are ready to seize the opportunity it offers, without the paralysing self-consciousness of their predecessors. Of course, the fact that you can build virtually anything now and nobody turns a hair – even Daniel Liebskind's Spiral project for the Victoria and Albert Museum in South Kensington, west London, no longer seems out of the ordinary – creates a climate in which sensationalism and shock tactics conform to the law of diminishing returns.

The rapid success of a generation of British artists now reaching early middle age wasn't exactly replicated in their architectural contemporaries. The overheads of practice are a lot higher for a start. But the two groups have clearly ended up doing quite a bit of creative cross fertilisation. When you are looking for an architect to extend your studio in Hoxton, east London, you inevitably find yourself rubbing up against a very specific approach to architecture in the neighbourhood – a process that could already be seen getting underway in the first edition of this book and which has moved several steps further since then. Think, for example, of David Adjaye's remarkable east London house for an artist couple and their young children completed in 2001.

The impact of digital technology has, of course, also transformed the practice of architecture, as it has of industrial design – two disciplines which themselves are also converging, both in their strategies and in the way in which practice has developed for a group of younger designers: coming together for specific projects, going their own way afterward, ready to combine competitions, exhibitions, publishing and design in one seamless operation. But the physical qualities of architecture still remain a powerful presence, one that is capable of maintaining architecture's place in a wider cultural dialogue. Even Koolhaas continues to practice, for all his protestations to the contrary, as an architect. He might find himself working with the team perfecting the software that will allow Prada customers to try on any item from its current collection without the need to remove any of their own garments, in the privacy of the new-style Prada virtual changing-room. But Prada went to Koolhaas not because he was a software designer or a retail designer but because he was an architect – a fact that meant, it hoped, he had capacity to formulate a bigger picture to help him to know what to do with all this technology stuff. So Koolhaas spends his time and energy producing books as thick as telephone directories about every project he works on, built or unbuilt, rather than fretting about the precision with which to turn a re-entrant corner. And as far as he sees it, these books are every bit as much a reflection of an architectural stance as any building. But he still has a profoundly architectural view of the world. It's architectural in its perspective, and architectural in the way that it attempts to synthesize complicated phenomena into a coherent perspective. It's a pattern that has had a pervasive influence, not just on the way that new architects work, but also on the nature of that work. The ability of the digital technologies to visualize architectural design has allowed the non-specialist client into the loop as never before. They can for the first time in history understand exactly what they are going to get before it's built.

Architecture is constantly changing, at a rate that is perhaps now faster than it has ever been. But it's also, in a sense, staying the same. The architect is given the chance to try to create a sense of order as if one perfectly proportioned, perfectly executed room can exist in the chaos of contemporary life. But architecture can also be the means with which to engage with popular culture. It is in a position to make clear connections between theory and practice. It is an activity that is far from pure. It is always open to contamination from other disciplines, partly because architects are such suckers for intellectual fads, and partly because they still, to an extent, labour under a certain inferiority complex. They constantly worry, deep down and in private, that they might not be quite serious enough.

Architecture is riddled with appealing contradictions that make it both worldly and unworldly. The architect is there to be taken advantage of and to take advantage. This is true not simply in the obvious sense of the commercial implications of architecture. Architecture now offers clients intellectual credibility, as well as direct economic advantage. It's tempting to see these activities as mutually exclusive, to see architecture becoming an increasingly atomized activity, a balkanized group of tribes. Some cling to traditional definitions of making architecture that involve careful logistics and a sense of the physical, others work on the margins between installation and performance art. Others again turn their skills with the screen and the keyboard to good use. It is tempting, but misleading. In the constantly mutating architectural climate in contemporary Britain, the apparently visionary can quickly be transformed into entirely practical. And vice versa. The rate of change and the constant exploration of new ways of practising architecture make complacency impossible. There has never been a moment when the enormously varied definitions of architecture have existed in such close proximity. Once it was possible to draw a clear line between architectural businessmen and architectural artists. Now it isn't. To survive, the big architectural practices have had to start to pay attention to the ideas that are emerging at the more experimental end of architectural practice, and those experimental practices are themselves being taken more seriously outside the professional hothouse. The competition for the future of the South Bank in London, for example, put Foreign Office Architects – a practice that featured in the first edition of this book, and whose largest realized commission to date is a restaurant (but who have the Yokohama Liner Terminal under construction) – on equal terms with the-hundred-strong practice of Rafael Vinoly. We are in the middle, not just of a generational shift, but probably also a paradigm shift about what architecture can be. The conventional notions of what constitutes mainstream architecture have been entirely transformed. At a time when architecture has begun to enjoy a wider audience, its own influences have also become more eclectic. Architects read more, they write more and they are interested in a much wider range of references, from Donald Judd to Derrida. Architecture has become a kind of cultural synthesis. The point about emerging architects is that they are not yet locked in stereotypes. They are finding their own voices as they experiment and explore. What they put forward are the prototypes for new approaches. In a context in which architecture is higher on the wider cultural agenda than it has ever been, they have an energy that promises to make Britain an increasingly visible architectural centre.

1|2 Elektra House,
Whitechapel,
London by Adjaye
and Associates.
A family home for
an artist couple and
their young children

Where are
they now?
Sophie Murray

The first edition of *New Architects* was published in 1998, the year Foster and Partners was voted the architects' favourite architect for the fourth consecutive year by readers of the *Architects Journal*, the British Library finally opened to the public, the Albert Memorial was unveiled after an £11m refurbishment and the Tate Modern was 'topped-out'.

It was the first book of its kind, more focused and informative than a practice directory, and more accessible, comprehensive and client-focused than academic surveys. The main reason for its conception was the often-voiced concern that many Lottery-funded projects were going to "architects over sixty", in the words of the former Secretary of State for the Environment, John Gummer. It was hoped that a survey of the best young architects in Britain would make all clients more aware of the possibilities offered by the new generation of practices.

So what has happened to the architects featured in the first book? Has the climate changed in their favour, or are the more experienced and established still being chosen over them. And how did inclusion in the book change their practices?

The practices featured in *New Architects* were a varied group. Some were very new, just one or two years old with little built-work behind them, and most of that residential work, interior conversions, extensions for friends of friends. Some of them were moving onto bigger projects, like galleries, office re-fits, retail and bar design. Some had been around for nearly ten years and had more built-work, with larger projects on the drawing board.

The level of experience and range of ages was different in each practice: some had moved from larger firms after only a few years in practice and some had moved from senior positions at well-established practices. Every firm fitted the same criteria as they have to fit for this edition: they were 'emerging' and talented, and they would benefit from the exposure provided by the book.

Some of the architects in the last book reappear in this edition because they have not yet secured that major commission that would confirm they are no longer 'emerging'. Entry into the book is a process of open competition, which was announced in the professional press, judged by a panel of experts and then each practice was visited by a team of independent assessors. Those practices that were featured in the

last book have been inspected before, and therefore the assessors' comments appear only on those practices that have been selected for *New Architects* for the first time. Some practices reapplied for inclusion in 2001 but were felt by the judges to have 'emerged'. Generally, practices have worked on bigger projects and have consolidated their position in particular fields with more built-work, more competition entries and wins, and more press coverage.

The first book was much appreciated by the architects who were included in it. Matthew Priestman of Matthew Priestman Architects commented that "it is very easy to use. The pictures are great and the text is clear and uniform". David McCall of OMI described it as a "comprehensive summary of what current architectural thinking is – and full of tasty images". Brian Vermeulen of Cottrell and Vermeulen said that he found that clients did use it when they were looking for an architect: "it is very, very useful". To Adam Zombory of Zombory Moldovan Moore "it was a very significant publication, people could get hold of it easily and internationally. One can also keep referring to it and keep showing it to people, because it doesn't instantly date like magazine articles do. We were aware of a lot of people having seen it. It was great that we were in it. It was very positive and an enormous help".

Wells Mackereth received twelve commissions directly as a result of the book's publication, and enjoyed a lot of related interest, particularly from those outside the world of architecture and design. David Sheppard's practice attracted the interest of the media, who he says use the book to find stories for style supplements and design sections. He was featured in several national Sunday supplements and was offered more work, including a gallery and retail scheme, as a result. The book has given Peter Barber's practice a significant boost: "We were desperate for a grant for a really exciting scheme in the East End of London and were despairing of ever getting funding. We were about to give up when the BBC phoned and said they had seen us in the book and asked if we had any interesting projects. It was through the BBC interest, as a result of the book, that we eventually got the funding we wanted. It is a brilliant book and keeps cropping up at just the right time".

Many architects said it gave the practice a great lift in the eyes of prospective clients and in the eyes of the architects themselves. According to Stephen Boyd of

Lee Boyd: "It helped us to build a profile as a practice with high standards and to develop new commissions with existing clients. It is a well-designed and respected book which is always in our reception for clients to flick through. We also showed it to the clients whose buildings were featured and it gave them enormous satisfaction". They also use it to show prospective clients that they are part of a group chosen for their talent, originality and commitment to high-quality design. This is echoed by many of the architects. Angela Brady of Brady and Mallalieu said: "reprints of our page in the directory have been a staple of our marketing brochures and client presentations, and we certainly believe the kudos of the listing has been an important and successful part of our marketing armoury. We are sure that being classed as one of 'Britain's best young architectural practices' has helped to increase our profile with potential clients".

David McCall said that it "sent the right messages out about the practice and carried a degree of kudos". Matthew Priestman said it is useful for "underpinning one's credibility", and Keith Williams, formerly of Pawson Williams, described it as "a showcase, the place to look for architects".

For Alex de Rijke of de Rijke Marsh Morgan, the main benefit of the book is that a practice is seen as eligible for invitations to competitions. When Brian Vermeulen went to see the British Council following an invitation to compete, there was copy on their table with post-it notes marking the pages of architects they were interested in. "Places like the British Council and CABE (Commission for Architecture and the Built Environment) have copies which they flick through when they are looking for a selection of architects for a competition," he said. David McCall saw the book as specifically targeted at organisations about to make Lottery applications, and OMI received a number of enquiries from such groups. Cottrell and Vermeulen have also received several invitations for competitions, which they believe to be a result of the book.

Many young practices compare the English competition system unfavourably with some European systems, such as Germany's, which allow young architects to compete on an even playing field with older and more experienced architects. There are very few open competitions in Britain, but on the Continent it is the norm when commissioning for public projects. The anonymity of the system means that a winner is chosen purely on the merit of that proposal, so young architects without a 'name' are often selected to design major public buildings. In turn, private clients do not always expect to see established practices carrying out bigger jobs and feel more comfortable commissioning younger, smaller firms. Michelle Cohen of Walters and Cohen suggested that selection procedures that require 'expressions of interest' at the first stage often militated against young practices. Those with little experience have less of a chance than those who can display examples of built work. "It is increasingly difficult for younger practices to get their foot in the door."

New Architects was certainly seen by many as an antidote to the problems encountered by new practices trying to break into new areas and build a varied portfolio. "It is a very useful way of putting young architects in a forum which is held by older architects who have strong positions in particular areas of work," according to David Sheppard. "It is these older architects who often get most of the jobs simply because people are unaware of the alternatives. The book gave the younger generation the opportunity to demonstrate the quality of work they are capable of and it has made a very positive contribution to the market."

One of the problems inherent in publishing completed works is the tendency for practices to be typecast. Since much of the work done by younger architects tends to be in residential, " the book should reflect not just what kind of work a practice is doing, but what it is capable of doing", said Jonathan Sergison of Sergison Bates. Alex de Rijke echoed this sentiment: "In this climate, architecturally and economically, many people use *New Architects* to find someone to do domestic extensions and refurbishments, and there's no harm in that, but young practices don't get to do anything else. It is important not to characterize young architects as those who do small, mostly domestic jobs, which do not help the practices to broaden their scope". Adam Zombory concurs: " If they see a house, they don't come to you with a gallery". He adds, however, that the book "helped to give clients confidence in what small practices can do".

New Architects tries to present the possibilities and potential of these younger architects, but it can only publish the material that is available from the practices. Peter Barber Architects, which was quite small in 1998, realized that if he presented just domestic work, the practice would risk being defined by that, so the entry

focused instead on masterplanning, and when the book ended up on the tables of clients in local government, they contacted him. He is now working on a large masterplanning and urban design scheme, for Hackney in east London, that will demolish two run-down housing estates and create a mixed-use development with shops, housing for 3000 people and a park. It is "at the sharp end" of the sort of projects proposed by architect Richard Rogers for the Government's Urban Task Force. It is a radical plan to transform a whole area and the lives of thousands of people, turning a problem into a new model for urban living.

Typecasting is a problem that can be solved by architects' own marketing strategies, but marketing is a concept that is treated with a mixture of suspicion and contempt by emerging architects. They think marketing is about 'cold calling', 'the hard sell' and 'endless mail-shots'. It is interesting to note that those architects who were most enthusiastic about *New Architects* are those who generally experience the most success. This is because they saw the book as a great opportunity and used it to promote themselves, rather than leaving it on the shelf and expecting commissions to come to them.

Despite these concerns about the difficulties faced by young practices, many of the 'New Architects' have won significant commissions over the last few years – a testament to how many clients are willing to look beyond limited experience and select less obvious and established designers. De Rijke Marsh Morgan had a school in Southwark, south-east London, worth £9.5m, at the pre-planning stage that was scheduled to be on site by the end of 2001. Lee Boyd built the European headquarters for Adobe Systems and won the RIBA Silver Medal in the Best New Building of 2000 category, and Mark Fisher Associates completed the building for BP Amoco's technical branch. Sergison Bates won a competition organized by the William Sutton Trust to design a prototype for affordable housing, and its semi-detached pair of houses has now been completed. On the basis of this win, it was shortlisted for a housing scheme in Shepherdess Walk for the new Islington and Hackney Housing Association in London, which it also won and has since completed. The ideas developed in the prototype have evolved into a current project for terraced housing in Essex. The practice has also been working on the masterplan for a university in Winterthur, Switzerland, and has a mixed-use development for Baylight Properties that is about to go on site in

Wandsworth, south-west London.

Snell Associates completed a new gallery in Surrey that won five design awards, it is the appointed architect of the Arnolfini in Bristol, it redeveloped the Theatre Royal in Gibraltar and is the architect for the £70m redevelopment of Fulham Football Club. Competition wins for Walters and Cohen included designing a new national photographic centre for Wales and a new concert hall and teaching studios at the Yehudi Menuhin School. It was also joint winner in the Sustainable Schools Competition and now has a great deal of experience in the education sector.

Since the publication of *New Architects*, Cottrell and Vermeulen has worked with Portakabin to design a mass-produced, pre-fabricated structure. The practice has won an invited competition to build post-graduate student accommodation for Churchill College, Cambridge, and is about to go on site. It also won an invited competition to design the Gilray exhibition at Tate Britain for June 2001. Liverpool-based practice Shed KM has nearly completed the conversion of Liverpool Collegiate School into ninety-six apartments for developers, Urban Splash, and the conversion of the 1917 'Bryant and May' match factory into modern business units. It is also strategic architect for the £80m redevelopment of Fort Dunlop and has just started work on a health centre in Ashby de la Zouche. Phase I of the refurbishment of Birmingham Repertory Theatre, which included the renovation of the main auditorium, has been completed by Keith Williams Architects. The job was worth £7.1m and was built in just 12 weeks. Keith Williams Architects is also the only UK architect to reach the final in the competition to design the 40,000 sq m Turin City Library in Italy.

Zombory Moldovan Moore designed a Jewish Cultural Centre near Marble Arch in central London, a gallery in Surrey, a hotel based on the Japanese module idea and a public outdoor performance space, in Saltaire, Yorkshire, that is connected to the Hockney gallery.

The teaching block and refectory for South Trafford College, Cheshire, due for completion in 2002, was designed by OMI, who has also completed the National Football Museum, which opened to the public in February 2001 and is set to become a national focus for the story of football. Located at the redeveloped Deepdale Stadium, the home of Preston North End Football Club, it was partly funded by the Heritage

Lottery Fund. OMI's other major project since the publication of *New Architects* is the Fourth Church of Christ Scientist in Manchester. It won an RIBA Award and an MSA Award in 1999 and has been extensively covered in the press.

Harrison Ince has completed phase two of the 'Homes for Change' project in Manchester. Its client was the Guinness Trust, who will eventually hand over the housing to the co-operative that helped Harrison Ince to design the buildings. It won an MSA Award in 2001 for a completed housing project – it was in the unbuilt category in 2000 – and it was shortlisted for an RIBA Award, also in 2001. It also designed a controversial scheme for Chester Arena, extending and expanding the buildings around the Roman amphitheatre. The practice has been working with Wetherspoon's since 1998 on the extensive expansion and modernization of its bars and pubs.

What else has changed for the now not-so-new architects since the publication of the book? Brian Vermeulen simply answered: "We were very poor when we went in that book and now we're not poor". This was true of most of those questioned, and it gives some hope to those architects in this book who despair of their bank balances. Sean Griffiths of FAT (Fashion Architecture Taste) says that since the book was published the practice is "more professional, more 'grown-up' and makes more money". The architects themselves are " a little bit more noused-up". In the past few years the reputation of the practice has really spread beyond what Griffiths sees as the narrow confines of the world of architecture. The practice was described in the first book as "a creative practice widely admired for its design, architecture and art output", and since then Griffiths says the practice has an even more varied output and relies less on building design. Work now includes what he calls "ambient media advertising" and other design, including furniture. "Much of our work is for advertising agencies, who ask us to design something for a specific campaign. Maybe a display for the product they are launching, or some kind of art event to support more traditional methods of advertising". The jobs are small compared to designing a building, but a great deal more lucrative, he says. The firm has created a definite profile and reputation for a particular kind of thinking in a niche market.

David McCall of OMI said that his practice has become more confident and focused in its particular view of architecture: "Time and experience have confirmed that our approach reaps dividends and is very well worth pursuing". Stephen Boyd said that Lee Boyd began to take on larger commissions and has been looking at other parts of the UK and abroad for expansion, while also broadening its range of services to include furniture and landscaping (they are currently working on a major eighty-acre site in Perthshire).

New Architects is used by students, both in Britain and abroad, who are looking for a job in a credible and exciting practice. For many of the firms, this is the main method of recruiting. Photographers send their portfolios and there was some talk about hotels using it as a mailing list to entice hip young architects into their bars. It is also of educational value: many architects pointed out that the public is bombarded with information about young artists, but it is hard to find similar information about young architects. For some of the architects themselves, *New Architects* created the idea of a group which defined the work of a generation. Adam Zombory said of the book: "It was a good eye-opener for the architectural profession, and for us, because it gave us all a sense of the great body of work that was being amassed by young architectural practices. It helped us to see what everyone else was up to and to focus on what we want to do".

The book is a reference guide for all those who want to use an architect, for journalists who want to know what's going on in architecture and for architects who want to check out the competition. Those who were featured in *New Architects* have clearly benefited from the range of people who now have access to information about their practices, and have used the few years to build their reputations, gain experience and broaden their horizons. The book defined them as a group who would have a significant impact on our built environment: they have, and will continue to do so.

How to be a
good client
Claire Melhuish

New Architects provided a formal, public launch pad for a new generation of architects battling to carve out and maintain a foothold in a hard-headed industry. Hampered by a lack of both contacts and track record in the various sectors, architects' early careers can be notoriously difficult, but this section, revisiting a handful of those practices featured in the original volume, shows evidence not only of the scope of new work carried out by previously little-known architects, but also of the enthusiasm and satisfaction of clients who initially, in many cases, felt they were taking a risk in overlooking a lack of past experience.

Many clients manifest a deep-seated fear of finding themselves burdened with an architect who seems incapable of listening to their requirements and concerns, and who is intent on designing according to their own agenda, riding roughshod over anyone else's thoughts and ideas. By all accounts, the myth of the arrogant, insensitive architect, spawned by Modernist ideology during the construction boom of the post-war years, lingers on. But the accounts of the clients who have availed themselves of the services – and insight – of a new generation of architects reveal the extent to which they give the lie to that myth. Nearly all the clients questioned professed themselves delighted and surprised at finding how open-minded, responsive and skilled many younger architects are at interpreting their needs and at dealing with the complex, multi-faceted relationships involved in bringing a building to fruition. In the words of one: "Many more-established architects simply do not make the effort to sustain a dialogue through the long, slow design and construction process". Another suggests that not only do "big name" architects often fail to respond to the client's requirements, but they also tend to show less respect for the practicalities of a project, such as the budget, and for a site's context.

But if this should suggest that today's young architects have become so self-effacing as to be incapable of delivering anything but a bland, insipid architecture stamped with the failure of vision and the triumph of pale compromise, this also would be a sad misrepresentation. The overwhelming verdict of clients seems to be that the younger and less experienced the architect, the more likely a stunning end result driven by a strong idea that really works. While not all would go so far as to admit to cynicism

about the ability of architects in general to produce any ideas at all, most concur that the building achieved through the architectural process surpassed their expectations of the possibilities, and sustains a strong, positive response from users. In the majority of cases it would seem that short-term risk is judged to have paid off handsomely in long-term investment, begetting a new generation of firmly rooted, culturally sustainable, living buildings.

Hawkins Brown

Client Adam Hart, Hackney Co-operative Developments
Project Bradbury Street managed workspace, Dalston, London

"The reason why so many inner city sites are blighted," says Adam Hart, "is because of the sheer complexity of local interests, bureaucracy and public-private sector relationships". But Hawkins Brown proved to be "crazy, skilled and committed enough" to push through the Bradbury Street project, resulting in the "only really significant intervention of good-quality Modernist design in this area". Hart says the fact that the architects were local and young generated "an empathy about where we stand". They had "the cheek and confidence" to produce an alternative to approved plans for demolition and rebuilding on the site with a "ghastly design-and-build" scheme, but they were also practical, professional, and diplomatic. Above all, they were willing to collaborate and consult. The resulting scheme, employing industrial-type solutions without turning the architecture into a manifesto for 'new brutalism', and using colour effectively, has been "universally acclaimed locally", says Hart, and has had a demonstrably positive effect in terms of publicity for the company. Most strikingly, the new tenants are "proud of their units and jealously guard them", and there has been no vandalism at all.

AHMM

Client Gordon Powell, Property Services Division, Essex County Council
Project Great Notley School, Essex

Perhaps AHMM's most impressive achievement on this project was to dissuade the developer building pastiche houses on all sides of the site from using its veto over their proposals for an eye-catching modern school in their midst. Powell says the scheme itself, which was to

provide a prototype for a model sustainable school, "was obviously very well thought-out, particularly in terms of its lighting, showing that when it comes to environmental performance you can do things by design".

Powell felt that the relative lack of experience of the design team in this particular sector might have prompted them to draw on the accumulated knowledge and experience of the client body more than it did, but on the other hand, he and his colleagues were impressed by the fact that they seemed happy to listen to suggestions and comments on the design. The building is acknowledged to be both a good piece of architecture and to work well as a school. "We took a gamble and it paid off," says Powell. But changes in the political climate on the client's side suggest it is unlikely to happen again.

Hodder Associates

Client Martin Jackson, Bursar, St Catherine's College, Oxford
Project St Catherine's College, phases 1 and 2, Oxford

Extending Arne Jacobsen's Grade 1 listed St Catherine's College was a very high profile job that the college awarded to Hodder Associates on the basis of comparatively little previous work. Jackson says it was the "great attention to detail", comparable to Jacobsen's own, that brought the practice to the college's notice. Subsequently, it feels not only gratified in taking that risk, but also "a slight sense of responsibility" for Hodder's growth and success since then.

The great strength of Hodder's scheme is that "most people recognize it immediately as a response to the Jacobsen buildings". Jackson also describes Phase 2, particularly the lecture-theatre element, as "a very clever design indeed". Hodder showed himself "very keen to meet the needs of the client", but he was also prepared to try things "that were right at the cutting edge of innovation in the industry at that time". This meant putting a certain amount of pressure on the contractors, and Hodder exhibited "great patience and not much give". Jackson admits this "is not the fastest way to get a building built … but it is the way to get quality architecture … if he'd diluted that approach he wouldn't be where he is now".

Niall McLaughlin Architects

Client Jill Theis, Pavilion Trust
Project Bandstand for the de la Warr Pavilion, Bexhill-on-Sea, 1999–2001

This was McLaughlin's first local authority job, and Theis says that the first planning meeting was "horrendous". But if some of the councillors "didn't think much" of his unusual design, Theis is convinced it will be very exciting.

The client didn't have a clear brief, but it did specify that the architect would be expected to work with schoolchildren during the design process. McLaughlin seemed to genuinely welcome the proposal and have a conviction about its worth. Theis felt that none of the more-established architects interviewed would have been able to respond in the way that McLaughlin has subsequently to that process. He demonstrated an innate ability to talk to the children, assess their models seriously and to go at their pace – indeed, the 'butterfly' design of the roof bears a close resemblance to their ideas. He was also "very sympathetic to the site and its challenges", and "worked with the staff of the [Pavilion] very well". Theis says McLaughlin succeeded in giving the client itself "a great sense of confidence", especially in the nerve-wracking run-up to initiating construction works on site.

Buschow Henley

Client George Michaelides
Projects Converted office and apartment

When media-and-marketing company Michaelides and Bednash set up in the mid-1990s, it wanted an office "that would do the marketing for the company".

It went to Simon Henley, who was only just setting up his own practice because it wanted, above all, somebody with ideas – and, suggests Michaelides, a lot of architects haven't really got many: "It's easy to put a skin on something but for it not to mean a lot and to disappear very quickly".

The company's intuition was rewarded in Henley's challenging scheme focused around "a very symbolic long table that really works". The brief asked for a design that would help create "a culture of teamwork" in the office, and Michaelides points out that six years later the firm still doesn't feel the need to redesign the office. Since then, the architects have gained a very strong reputation in the marketing and media world. In this case, the strength of the architectural idea overrode any questions raised about the practice's level of experience.

McDowell & Benedetti

Client John Penton, Merchant Taylors Company
Project Mulberry House nursing home, Lewisham

John Penton first met McDowell and Benedetti in their role as accessibility consultants on the practice's short-listed Millennium Bridge proposal. It was the open-minded quality of the firm's approach that led him to suggest its appointment as architect for redevelopment of part of the Lewisham estate, in spite of the lack of a significant track record,

Penton identifies the key characteristics of the practice as a receptiveness to the client, and "a real passion for good architecture … a distinctive design ethos which they bring to the job". The design of the new nursing home is "uncompromising – it doesn't make any gestures to pastiche at all". But it was also developed in the context of "an impeccable local consultation process", during which one of its most implacable opponents conceded that the architects had done a good job. The effect has been to encourage Merchant Taylors to re-evaluate its strategy for the Lewisham estate and to use feasibility studies by MacDowell and Benedetti for several further sites.

Malcom Fraser

Client Tessa Ransford, founder and first director, Poetry Library
Project Poetry Library, Edinburgh

Malcom Fraser was a one-man practice and "quite inexperienced" when it started work on the Lottery application for this project, so Ransford appointed a project manager to supervise the construction. But he had a "dream of building something modern and fitting" in the Old Town, and he set his students the task of designing a new poetry library as a hypothetical project, based on Ransford's own brief.

Fraser was also instrumental in identifying the site for the new building. Ransford was concerned it was too far off the beaten track, but Fraser's insight has been vindicated by the building of the new Parliament building alongside. When the Arts Council's representatives saw the completed library, they were stunned. Ransford describes it as "inspired". The advantage of working with Fraser and project architect Neil Simpson was that "every detail" was discussed as they went along. She regards the completion of the new building as symbolizing the start of a new era in the library's history.

Ian Simpson

Client Fran Toms, Manchester City Council Special Projects
Project Urbis exhibition centre, Manchester

Nine months away from completion of the £30m Urbis exhibition centre in central Manchester, Fran Toms says the building will be a landmark project that will help Manchester to reposition itself as an international and European city. This is due largely to its architecturally innovative character, and also to the fact that Ian Simpson knows Manchester well, and "works with the city's interests at heart".

Of the design's presentation, she remembers that "the panel was very excited". It has hardly been altered since then. Toms describes Simpson as being "among the most innovative and talented architects". His "particular hand on a project" makes a significant difference, and he maintains a personal involvement throughout. In terms of resolving problems, "it usually comes down to a personal discussion between him and me", she says, but he always attends critical meetings and is "young enough not to have the arrogance of more established clients – he still listens". "In the end," she says, "these guys are passionate about what they want".

Harper McKay

Client Jeremy Sinclair, M&C Saatchi
Project Headquarters, Golden Square, London

M & C Saatchi picked Harper MacKay four or five years ago "because they had the quickest grasp as to what feel we wanted the building to have". The client had no previous knowledge of the practice, or many others beyond the Rogers-Foster constellation, but it did have a very clear idea about what it wanted to do. "We emptied the building, built all the walls out of glass, and put an atrium down the middle," says Sinclair. Harper Mackay's "cleverness", he thinks, must be in "seeing what people want" – because none of its buildings seem to be the same. "We have views about the appearance and design of things," Sinclair explains, and Harper Mackay was good at taking those on board and realizing them well. They were also good at "steering us off other things".

The company was "absolutely delighted" with the result of the architects' intervention, and was impressed by its effect on users and visitors. People use the atrium foyer-and-café area to work in, and clients like it so much that they frequently hire it for their own functions.

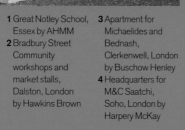

1 Great Notley School, Essex by AHMM

2 Bradbury Street Community workshops and market stalls, Dalston, London by Hawkins Brown

3 Apartment for Michaelides and Bednash, Clerkenwell, London by Buschow Henley

4 Headquarters for M&C Saatchi, Soho, London by Harpery McKay

Directory

51% Studios
1–5 Clerkenwell Road
London EC1M 5PA
T   020 7251 6962
F   020 7267 6964
E   info@51pct.com
W   www.51pct.com

51% Studios

Formed in 1995, this is a multi-disciplinary practice whose projects, theoretical and realized, have spanned architecture, furniture, industrial design and graphics, landscape and urban strategy.

The principals are also involved in publications, exhibitions and digital technology. One of the practice's largest projects is a £7.5m centre for the arts for Sterts Council, Devon, where it took its design cue from the existing courtyard of an old farm and created a hierarchy of protected and connected courtyards, ideal for the extreme landscape of Bodmin Moor. A granite-and-glass 'crystal court' at the centre of the scheme provides a winter garden and performance space.

Current projects include the conversion and extension of a private house in Chiswick, west London, and the design of video-editing facilities in Soho, central London.

51% Studios has worked on a surprisingly diverse range of architectural projects, each managed to a high creative standard. The practice's perception of what can be achieved in response to a brief is highly imaginative. An example is 'designing in' the use of reflected sunlight.

This level of detailed thinking is evident throughout the practice's work. Idiosyncratic features range from the inversion of a traditional staircase in the rebuilding of a house in Highgate, north London, to the "warmed-up minimalist lining" of a Victorian house in Chiswick, west London.

A responsive interest in the possibilities of existing buildings, and a readiness to think long-term (including environmentally) are key aspects of the firm's ethos.

2

1|2 PW Search and
Select offices,
Clerkenwell, London

1

4

3|4 The Greenhouse,
Dartmouth Park,
London

5th Studio

5th Studio
Darkroom
Gwydir Street
Cambridge CB1 2LJ
T   01223 516009
F   01223 566010
E   mail@5thstudio.co.uk

5th Studio has grown rapidly in range and scale since its foundation in 1997, and the directors express a desire not to limit themselves to specialization in any one area, although it started, like many young practices, with small-scale extensions and remodelings.

The directors say that their architecture is both a "propositional" and a "prospective" activity that has encouraged the office to invent projects on a larger scale than the small domestic work usually available. 5th Studio is a design-led practice that takes great pride in its energetic and innovative approach to architecture and urban design.

The key to the practice's approach lies in the creation of inspired settings for contemporary life. Current projects, including a £3.5m hostel for students with disabilities for Cambridge University, indicate a move into a broader range of commissions.

The amalgamation of Oliver Smith's experience of signature practices and Tom Holbrook's origins in film and television design has produced a firm with great design talent and an impressive output.

Its approach to projects is innovative and imaginative, and the quality of work produced is high. The built work suggests a strong affinity with the client and it achieves imaginative lived-in spatial solutions, coupled with fresh and well-crafted detailing. What is most striking about 5th Studio, apart from its general standard of design confidence and competence, is its entrepreneurial, pro-active stance.

1

1 Bridget's House for Disabled Students, Cambridge and Anglia Universities

2 Refurbishment, Courtnell Street, London

3 Staircase, Eden Street, Cambridge

2

ACQ
26 Mortimer Street
London W1N 7RA
T   020 7436 4866
F   020 7636 3396
E   info@acq-architects.com
W   www.acq-architects.com

ACQ

The partners at ACQ – Avery Agnelli, Kim Quazi and Hal Currey – all worked at Richard Rogers Partnership before setting up their own practice, and they draw on their experience of big-building culture to tackle projects on a range of scales.

Though work to date has been made up of smaller commercial and private residential projects, ACQ is currently working on some much larger sites. It has completed a number of high-profile jobs, the most prominent of which was the interior of clickmango.com's meeting room in Brick Lane, east London. With its use of inflatable screens, the design highlights the practice's experimental credentials and it was widely featured in the national media.

The practice is keen to use both traditional materials and those that are used less often in an architectural context, such as PVC, rubber and leather.

ACQ aims to provide thoughtful design for modern living without employing an intrusive house style. Solutions grow from the demands of the client and the location; and the result often surprises the designers.

This competent and thoughtful practice is producing work that is ground-breaking, practical and fun. It uses excellent models and colourful sketches to explain its intentions in a sympathetic and clear manner. Good communication with other professionals and contractors is central to the practice's success; evaluating past work informs the future. Sustainability is seen as a fundamental part of building design.

2

1

1|2 Reception island,
Marakon offices,
London

3 Air-cooling system,
Channel 5
Television, London

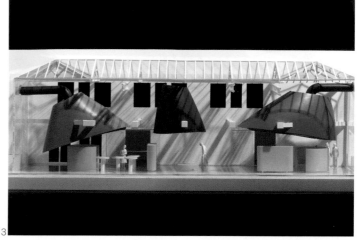

3

4

5

4 Bar, Channel 4
Television, London
5 Restaurant, Channel 4
Television, London

Adams & Sutherland
Studio 3c, Highgate Business Centre
33 Greenwood Place
London NW5 1LB
T 020 7267 1747
F 020 7482 2359
E info@adams-sutherland.co.uk
W www.adams-sutherland.co.uk

Adams & Sutherland

Elizabeth Adams and Graeme Sutherland collaborated on a number of projects before setting up practice in 1997 after winning the Will Adams Centre competition. The majority of their projects focus on the social and environmental aspects of architecture, and they state a commitment to social change via architecture as the main motivation of their practice.

They are particularly interested in the sensory experience of a place, the result of which can be seen in the garden wilderness of the Evergreen Adventure Playground in Hackney, east London. Their original vision for the playground was "an integrated environment for excitement, curiosity and adventure". They describe their buildings as having "an in-between quality" which often juxtaposes radically different interests and needs, characterising their work as "fragmentary rather than finite".

New projects include a special-needs arts centre in Hastings, East Sussex, for which they have taken time to understand the kinds of complex physical and mental difficulties experienced by the centre-users. They also see the regeneration of an area with such serious social deprivation as a key part of the project.

A practice with a considerable track record in maintaining a clear and sensitive – often rather magical – design approach, on very tough, long-running projects for public and private clients. It is good at dealing with socially, and financially, complex projects and its insistence on understanding the project-users' needs is notable.

The work shows no sign of compromise, producing surprising beauty in unlikely places. The schemes offer pleasure and imaginative scope in extremely tough circumstances.

1|2 Mixed-use conversion, Dorking, Surrey
3|4 Evergreen Adventure Playground, Hackney, London

2

3

1

AEM
80 O'Donnell Court
Brunswick Centre, Brunswick Square
London WC1N 1NX
T 020 7713 9191
F 020 7713 9199
E a-em@dial.pipex.com
W www.a-em.com

AEM

AEM's approach is based on Modernist principles and embraces a cultural and environmental agenda that reflects the reality of contemporary living patterns. It also addresses concerns about the future of energy and material resources. The practice believes that fluid communication between all parties concerned is the only way to achieve its particular brand of lateral thinking and to produce the most appropriate and life-enhancing design solutions.

The practice has established a reputation for architecture characterized by transparency, lightness and economy of means. Its approach repeatedly challenges the spatial possibilities that initially seem to be available. The design is informed by a sense of restraint and control, overlaid by a vibrant palette of materials, form and colour. The practice works on projects on a variety of scales, from furniture to new-build and refurbishment in the residential, commercial, office and leisure sectors.

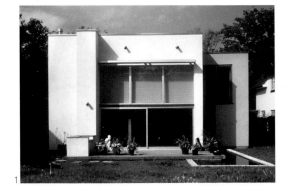

1|2 New-build house,
World's End Lane,
Orpington, Kent

3 Entrance space,
National Maritime
Museum, Greenwich,
London

4|5 Two-storey
structure, Swan's
Nest, Middle
Chedworth,
Gloucestershire

Alan Jones Architects
84 Main Street
Randalstown, Antrim
Belfast BT41 3BB
T   02894478058
F   02894478059
E   admin@jonesarchitects.com
W www.jonesarchitects.com

This very new practice has been established within the last two years. In its first year it won the regional RIBA Award for an addition to a farmhouse, and it has been honoured several times since. Jones previously worked for Michael Hopkins for seven years, and for David Morley for three years, before returning to Ireland to set up his own practice.

The practice's design approach has been the subject of many articles in the general and professional press and has been covered in several exhibitions. Its investigation into a new Northern Irish design is described as "a discourse on the balance between utility, functionality and simplicity, with the constrained, abstract and elegant, to form a new plain style which echoes the architecture and design of previous eras of Ireland". The approach is contemporary in striving for a simplicity and calm that resonates with a desire for separation from the complexity of modern life.

Alan Jones Architects' work to date pursues an architecture of reduction – simple forms and spaces combine against a measured and assured awareness of the context. The practice's two domestic projects can be read as critiques of the Ulster rural dwelling – the extension to the house at Cranfield abstracts the language of typical farm out-buildings, presenting itself as a muted zinc container against which the existing house is reviewed. Conversely, the house at Newry draws more obviously on a vernacular vocabulary to offer a more laconic and measured characterisation. Both schemes are founded in a healthy understanding of their respective patterns of occupation, offering practical and enriching internal space. The work of the practice is underpinned by a clear sense of refinement of simple themes and components – even under modest budgets there is a sense of precision and particularity, which is especially apparent in the elements of furniture designed by the practice.

2

1 Residential new-
  build, Lislea, Newry,
  Co. Down,
  Northern Ireland

2|3 Residential
  extension, Cranfield,
  Randalstown,
  Co. Antrim,
  Northern Ireland

1

3

Alastair Howe Architects
50 Tanner's Way
Hunsdon Wharf
Herts. SG12 8QF
T   01279 439 640
E   alastair@alastairhowe.co.uk

Alastair Howe Architects

Space and light are central to
Alastair Howe's architectural vision,
examples of which can be seen in
the mostly private residential and
small commercial projects the
practice has undertaken since
its formation in 1993. Howe is an
ecologically-conscious architect
who avoids a complex high-
maintenance, high-cost approach,
leaning instead towards low-tech
simplicity. He achieves this by
designing spaces where the
environmental control is at the hand
of the user and is inherent in the
building. The long-term, rather
than the immediate, is his prime
consideration; a factor which is
particularly important in residential
projects. He is dedicated to quality
contemporary design and is
determined to solve the complex
design problems presented by
refurbishments and modern
projects in traditional residential
areas. The firm has been featured
extensively in both the national
and trade press, and work has
been exhibited in various venues,
including the RIBA and the CUBE
gallery in Manchester.

1|3 Residential
    conversion,
    St John's Wood,
    London
2|4 Residential
    conversion,
    Camden, London

4

Alison Brooks Architects
35 Britannia Row
London N1 8QH
T 020 7704 8808
F 020 7704 8409
E info@abaspace.com

Alison Brooks Architects

Alison Brooks founded ABA in 1996 after a six-year partnership with Ron Arad. The work ranges from urban design, housing and landscapes to commercial interiors and private residential projects.

ABA is recognized for producing an experimental yet accessible architecture perhaps best known to the general public as Belgo Centraal and Belgo Noord restaurants in London. *Architectural Design* magazine has praised the practice's "ability to see the full implications of a scheme within its urban setting".

The practice states that each of its projects becomes "a collaboration between experience and desire, open to instinct and invention". A key focus of the practice's ethos is the necessity of resolving complex design problems outside of precedent – a process which they term 'reframing' or 'unframing'. As the architects themselves explain: "Within this 'unframework', humour slides into the work – humour being an emotion that reaches across the boundaries of role and expectation".

ABA has a very organized office. The practice has great projects and very imaginative ideas and concepts that are clearly followed through in the execution of a project.

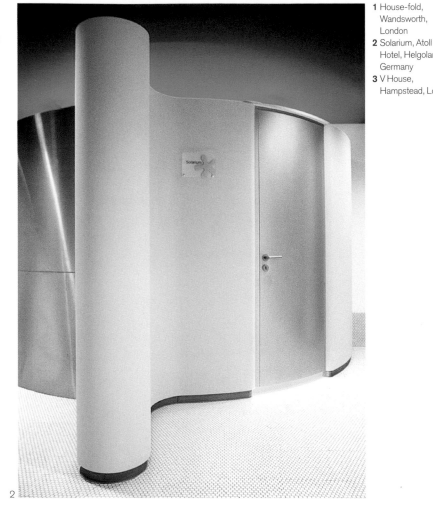

1 House-fold, Wandsworth, London
2 Solarium, Atoll Hotel, Helgoland, Germany
3 V House, Hampstead, London

2

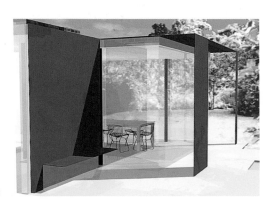

1

Arca
Ducie House
Ducie Street
Manchester M1 2JW
T   0161 236 6886
F   0161 236 5775
E   mail@arca.uk.com
W   www.arca.uk.com

Arca

Arca's design ethos springs from a dialogue with the problems it identifies within contemporary design philosophy. These problems include an over-emphasis on the theory behind a building and a lack of understanding of the public perception of architecture.

Its response is to focus on creating a connection between the social and spatial aspects of architecture. The materials used describe the history of the building, the area and the people who have used it. Another aspect of Arca's work is the development of flexible responses to the use of space.

Launched in 1998, within six months it had been commended in the RIBA/Urban Splash Britannia Basin Competition, and in 2000 it was a runner-up in both the Young Architectural Practice of the Year Award and the Young Architect of the Year Award. Schemes currently under development include a factory in Manchester and the Castlefield Gallery, also in Manchester.

Arca's work reveals a recurring theme of counter-position of new form with existing volume/container. This is most clearly seen in the Atomic Nightclub in Ashton-under-Lyne and the Box Works loft interior in Manchester.

The scale of the practice's work is gradually increasing and reflects its interest in a range of work from architecture to product design. The work was professionally presented and the practice demonstrated a commitment to the development of a clearly articulated formal progression.

1 Chorlton Park
Housing
Competition,
Manchester
2|3 Showflat,
Box Works,
Manchester

4

5

5 Atomic Nightclub,
Ashton-under-Lyne

Ash Sakula Architects
38 Mount Pleasant
London WC1X OAN
T   020 7837 9735
F   020 7837 9708
E   info@ashsak.demon.co.uk

Ash Sakula Architects

Set up in 1994 by Robert Sakula and Cany Ash, this practice has a varied list of clients which includes theatres, universities, large multi-national companies, advertising agencies and public authorities.

One of their earliest projects, The Birdwing Conservatory, was the smallest project ever to win a RIBA Award, but they have since gone on to much larger schemes and current work includes student flats in Brighton, two office conversions in central London and several sizeable private houses.

Both partners teach at various university Schools of Architecture, and they back up their commercial success with a sound design philosophy. They like their work to have a strong character, and in their many projects have explored the relationship between anonymity and autonomy, community and co-operation in their investigation of the urban environment.

Their professional confidence comes from their ability to take on complex challenges, and they pride themselves on using appropriate materials and techniques. Ash Sakula focus on the detailed atmosphere and texture of a place to create a design that has absorbed all the signals from the location, the environment and the potential users.

The principals are experienced and have good interpersonal skills, with a particular knowledge of the art world. The successful conversion of a 19th-century boiler house for Royal Holloway, University of London, was made possible by Ash Sakula's careful research into the needs of the users and clever resolution of technical issues. 'Hathouse' for Freeform, in Hackney, east London, reveals the practice's skills in building client confidence by setting up an effective team of consultants. Ash Sakula assess priorities and meet the challenge of technical complexity.

1|2 Office conversion, New Mill, Witney, Oxfordshire

1

2

3 Staircase, Camden,
London

4|5 Conservatory,
Islington, London

Avci + Jurca
35 Britannia Row
London N1 8QH
T 020 7226 1911
E selcuk@avcijurca.co.uk

Avci+Jurca

Selcuk Avci and Sanja Jurca set up this practice in 1997. Since then, the projects they have worked on have been wide-ranging, from the insertion of a shower room in a Victorian house to work on an international airport. Their work has been commissioned by universities, public authorities, museums and private clients.

Common to all the practice's projects is an ability to integrate a complete range of disciplines: art, architecture, ecology, science, engineering and economics. It places low-energy, environmentally sensitive design at the forefront of its agenda, and has a strong track record and reputation in the area of energy-conscious design. It works with leading engineers, environmental specialists and ecologists to achieve the balance it sees as vital to any architectural project. "A building as an organism is a consumer of nature's resources and has to be designed to give as much as it takes."

Current projects include two restaurants and offices for a firm of surveyors in Clerkenwell, east London. The practice is also involved in set design with theatres such as Sadler's Wells in London and the RSC in Stratford.

Incredibly varied work and typical of an emerging practice. They are very enthusiastic and seem to have a good team relationship within the office. The design ideas are imaginative and fun and the built projects look well executed with attention to detail.

1 Kotoka international airport, Japan (in association with TPS Consult)
2|3 British Telecom office, Mondial House, London (in association with TPS Consult)

4|5 Exsa textile
showroom, London

Bareham Meddings
Studio One
30–34 Aire Street
Leeds LS1 4HT
T   0113 245 7090
F   0113 245 7090
E   info@barehammeddings.com

Bareham Meddings

Bareham Meddings is "concerned with architecture as a poetic situation and with the human experience of place". Using this statement as a base it creates architecture which is informed at every level, from the broad strategy to the smallest detail, by the wish not to restrict the desires or aspirations of those involved in the project.

A major aid to the effectiveness of their design process is the use of the most up-to-date computer-aided design technology and the focus on personal commitment and contact. Current projects include several innovative residential projects, such as two new sustainable houses that share and revive a 'brownfield' site near Bradford, West Yorkshire, and a private house in Leeds, West Yorkshire, in which a glazed extension liberates a formerly cellular plan and acts as an environmental modifier for the entire house. The recently completed Trafford Ecology Centre in Manchester, commissioned by the Groundwork Trust, won the RIBA Manchester Design Award in both 1999 and 2000, and it was shortlisted for the RIBA National Awards.

1 Promenade,
competition,
Saltburn-by-the-Sea
2 Student Union,
Huddersfield
University

3 Northern Ballet
Theatre, competition,
Leeds

3

4

4 Hitman-Eddy
residence,
Lancashire
5 Trafford Park
Ecology Centre,
Manchester

5

Bauman Lyons Architects
15 Hawthorn Road
Leeds LS7 4PH
T   0113 294 4200
F   0113 294 1234
E   architects@baumanlyons.co.uk
W   www.baumanlyons.co.uk

Bauman Lyons Architects

This Leeds-based practice was established in 1992, and its projects have included arts venues, residential, offices, restaurants and bars as well as exhibition design, urban design and artist collaborations. All its work is informed by the belief that architecture can be meaningless, unless it fits well within an overall strategic urban and social context. This is particularly reflected in the volume of regeneration strategies the practice has been developing recently. The partners like to experiment with the collaborative process, and have worked with artists, writers, sculptors, graphic designers and photographers on a number of projects. This collaboration frees them from the temptation to fall back on standard solutions, and encourages them to push themselves to more extensive investigation, creating original designs. They are very conscious, however, of the need for good management to ensure that strong design is implemented without any loss of strategic vision. The practice is currently handling ten live projects, which range from a bus shelter to a private flat conversion.

This is a deeply committed practice, anxious to achieve good design, and the partners strive hard for that goal. They are committed to working with, and contributing to, the local community and committed to social and environmental sustainability.

The team uses models to explore and present ideas, which enables clients to see the design clearly. The practice also appreciates that a client can contribute towards a good design and a strong solution. As winning the Leeds Award for Architecture indicates, the practice knows there are three parties involved in the design process: the client, the principal contractor and the architect.

1 Metro bus stops, Bradford
2 South Promenade, Bridlington, Yorkshire
3|5 Yorkshire Sculpture Park, Wakefield

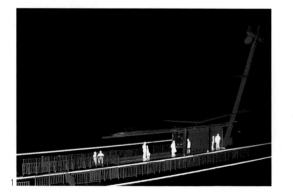

4 Media Centre,
Leeds

4

5

49

Botschi Vargas Architects
1 Addison Place
London W11 4RJ
T   020 7565 8319
F   020 7565 5588
E   botschivargas@netscapeonline.co.uk

Botschi Vargas Architects

This new practice has an unusual amount of experience, as both directors have worked in very senior positions in the offices of some of the best-known and respected international architects.

Pierre Botschi worked on projects such as the conversion of the former Billingsgate Market in the City while he was a director of the Richard Rogers Partnership. Luz Vargas has worked at KPF and Nicholas Grimshaw and Partners. The schemes they cover now range from small refurbishments and new-builds to hotels and community centres.

One of their largest ongoing projects is a £50m science, arts, technology and leisure centre in Cartagena, Colombia. Their main aim is to provide their client base with a strong and personalised design service with an emphasis on creating innovative, modern and timeless environments that are competitive on the financial market.

They are committed to combating the problems they see in today's architecture: a loss of soul, a lack of flexibility and the detrimental procurement methods that are inherent in the current construction industry.

A relatively new practice with a lot of major experience from previous practices. It has a very hands-on approach. Its friendly office is a two-storey, interconnected studio and residence, which makes a strong design statement.

With two principals and three staff the practice is well able to handle the considerable current workload and future projects of similar value. They have a strong design ethos.

1 Erco offices, Dover Street, London
2 BBC TV Centre, competition, White City, London
3 2000 Concept House, Ideal Home Exhibition, London

4|5 House refurbishment,
London

Boyarsky Murphy Architects
64 Oakley Square
London NW1 1NJ
T   020 7388 3572
F   020 7387 6776
E   n2@boyarskymurphy.com
W   www.boyarskymurphy.com

Boyarsky Murphy Architects

Boyarsky Murphy sees practice as an opportunity to build and to explore a range of wider issues that include design research, material investigations, urban studies, competitions and academic experimentation.

It is committed to exploring the use and possibilities for all kinds of materials. It expresses a desire to bring new and unfamiliar materials into the domestic environment as a focus of its material studies. The practice has worked on a range of projects: small residential refurbishments, additions and new-builds as well as large-scale housing studies. Projects have also included urban design projects and studies for a number of large cities in England and abroad.

Both partners are editors of Black Dog Press's series of books that highlight the working processes of younger architects around the world.

1 Community Centre, prototype, Denmark
2 Residential refurbishment, Holland Park, London
3 The Nook, Eel Pie Island, Twickenham

Bucholz McEvoy Architects
30 Bedford Street
Belfast BT2 7FF
Northern Ireland
T   02890 231170
F   02890 231169
E   mbucholz@indigo.ie
W   www.indigo.ie-mcevoy-index.html

Bucholz McEvoy Architects

This practice states an awareness of the contextual individuality of each project as the most important factor in creating an effective design solution. Context is understood as a complex set of interrelating factors: the place is the physical context, the function is the programatic context and the society is the cultural context. The practice considers economic and technological context as examples of possible limits.

No context is considered more important than another, but they all work together, exerting influence on a design. Dynamic leadership is the spark for innovation within the team and a diverse skill base develops strategies and solutions.

Communication is a priority, both during the design process, with the client, and after the completion of the project, communicating the achievements of the particular scheme to expert and non-expert audiences alike. The practice is a leader in sustainable design in Ireland and is committed to designing environmentally conscious work.

The clarity and richness of Bucholz McEvoy's work is hard-won through continual refinement and reassessment in pursuit of a cohesion where all components of a scheme are measured to serve the primary strategies.

An intense deliberation over construction and detail is a central theme characterizing the practice's work – all elements seem to be treated with this close scrutiny. An understanding of the processes of the manufacture as well as assembly has allowed the practice to cultivate a language inextricably linked with the 'making' of buildings. With another county civic building commencing on site this year, Bucholz McEvoy is setting itself up as one of the most important practices at work in Ireland.

1

1 The Welcoming
  Pavilions, Government
  Buildings, Dublin,
  Ireland
2|3 Fingal County Hall,
  Dublin, Ireland

2

C2 Architects
4 Candover Street
London W1W 7DJ
T   020 7580 8015
F   020 7580 8016
E   design@c2architects.demon.co.uk
W www.c2architects.com

C2 Architects

C2's project base is in inner London, where the firm mainly refurbishes, extends and converts existing structures, making them suitable for future use. The partners believe that there is no reason why a building should be derelict: it may no longer be useful for its original purpose, but its suitability for another should always be investigated, with demolition being considered a last resort. Along with a commitment to preservation, the practice posses an enthusiasm for energy conservation and sustainability.

It is adept at retaining the original feel of a building while adding a modern edge. This is demonstrated particularly well by the challenging redevelopment of Eagle House, a 1960s office block in Holborn, central London. The idea was to enhance the pedestrian-level environment and increase the presence of the building.

As well as larger-scale office developments, C2 has designed a modern interior, incorporating a glass bathtub and matching sink, for a penthouse apartment in Clerkenwell, east London.

This practice specializes in taking large projects to the planning approval stage. Projects are then generally carried out by a design and build contractor, with the architects acting as ongoing client advisors. Two major clients have provided substantial repeat contracts – for offices and for restaurants. This has included refurbishment work and major extensions. The practice provides innovative and sensitive solutions, often delivered in delicate situations. Design information is clearly communicated to clients with computer imaging and models.

1|3 Office conversion,
    Clerkenwell, London
2|4 Office conversion
    and extension,
    Barbican, London

Cartwright Pickard
16 Regents Wharf
All Saints Street
London N1 9RL
T   020 7837 7023
F   020 7837 7192
E   mail@cartwrightpickard.com

Cartwright Pickard

The experienced team at Cartwright Pickard has worked on a wide variety of projects, including the master planning of office parks, major mixed-use urban developments, large-scale commercial office buildings in the City of London, performing-arts projects and residential developments.

The design and construction of the workplace is a particular strength, as all the senior members of the practice have worked on several award-winning office buildings. The practice is dedicated to creating an integrated design approach that carefully co-ordinates the client, specialists, consultants and contractors involved.

This approach includes carrying out rigorous analysis of site and brief, and a thorough exploration of all relevant factors before commencing design work. The practice is currently developing projects that employ innovative prefabrication production engineering in their construction and has considerable experience in low-energy and sustainable building design.

1 Musicians' Institute,
  London
2 Riverdale Business
  Park, Fall Ings,
  Wakefield

3|4 Murray Grove, social
housing, Peabody
Trust, London

Charles Barclay Architects
74 Josephine Avenue
London SW2 2LA
T 020 8674 0037
F 020 8683 9696
E cba@cbarchitects.co.uk
W www.cbarchitects.co.uk

Charles Barclay Architects

Charles Barclay believes in engaging with the location of a project both in terms of aesthetics and in terms of social and environmental responsibility.

The practice "rejects the notion of tabula rasa and the naïve utopian fantasies of futuristic imagery", and it builds modern structures that interact sensitively with their historical surroundings. It is committed to producing well-detailed modern design and adheres to two main principles: the appreciation of the value of a collaborative approach and the necessity of experimentation.

The practice also builds models of most of its projects, to test ideas and allow greater communication with clients and within the office. It is interested in laterally-conceived strategies for re-habitation in the city, an example of which can be seen in its offices, which were converted from a workshop in a run-down part of Brixton, south London. It believes in the importance of public architecture and aspires to acquire projects in the public realm.

As principal, Charles Barclay makes all the main design decisions on commissioned work: clients insist that they expect him to lead design, especially since all the work so far is for domestic owner-occupiers. Barclay emphasises that when the practice is involved in a competition all contributions are considered and debated.

The office is a single-storey converted workshop and everyone works in the same large, simple, white space, which is obviously convenient and appropriate for teamwork.

The quality of design approach and detail showed the expertise and pleasure Barclay and his team have in their work, although the practice is keen to work on other building types. A proposal for an addition to a listed Georgian house in Blackheath, south London, revealed respect for the existing structure while providing it with a thoroughly modern extension.

2

1 Conversion, Winson, Gloucestershire
2 Residential refubishment, Hampstead, London
3|4 Residential refurbishment, Blackheath, London

3

1

4

Clash Associates
109 Bridge House
Three Mills Island, Three Mills Lane
London E3 3DU
T   020 8215 3360
F   020 8215 3490
E   pc@clashassociates.demon.co.uk

Clash Associates

Clash Associates has worked with the private sector, regeneration agencies and with local authorities on projects that include a number of lottery-funded schemes. It has had experience designing offices, galleries and exhibitions, schools, housing, urban planning and landscape. It has special experience in transport and engineering projects, particularly bridges.

The starting point for any project is a visual concept that is backed by an interest in a technical idea or in a set of rules particular to each scheme. The projects work from an architectural position towards a fusion of architecture and engineering.

The element of 'discovery' in the practice's work is strong, as both engineering and architectural boundaries are stretched. Peter Clash has worked with Foster and Partners in Hong Kong and until 1994, when he founded his practice, he was Associate Partner at Alsop and Störmer. Current projects include a submission for a new Student Union building at the University of Rennes in France.

Clash works on relatively large proposals and has done little or no domestic work. He often works closely with engineers and says he wants to "aestheticize structure". A theme of civil engineering runs through his work.

1 Bridge, Three
  Mills, London
2 Landscaping,
  Three Mills,
  London
3|4 Bus station,
    Spijkenisse,
    Netherlands

D – Squared Design
Studio H
Eden Mews
56 Eden Grove
London N7 8EG
T 020 7609 0931
F 020 7700 6044
E dsquared@globalnet.co.uk

D–Squared Design

This firm was formed in 1994 and has since then been involved in a wide range of design projects. Its architecture focuses on sustainability, and particularly the invention of energy-efficient construction processes.

Projects at the single building scale pay careful attention to the use of daylight and the management of energy-flows within structures. In larger-scale urban proposals, such as for Colombo in Sri Lanka, more complex infrastructural propositions for sustainability have been explored. The partners' belief that sophisticated forms of multi-disciplinary co-operation and understanding are essential for new urban solutions underpins these projects.

The firm itself is an example of the multi-skilled approach necessary for successful twenty-first-century design solutions. Its installations are a combination of video and architectural techniques that create dynamic three-dimensional events and include interactive and acoustic elements. The product design, particularly the gazebo and springseat, has received a great deal of both trade and national press interest.

This practice combines sustainable architecture with product design, video and installation art. The mix of skills is dynamic and unexpected. Clearly the practice's unique strength lies in the area of architecture and sustainability.

Backed by substantial and well-respected research, the practice creates work with social integrity. It addresses urgent issues of sustainability at both the urban and the building scale. It does so with refreshing clarity, sensuality and playfulness.

The combination of such wide-ranging capabilities in the service of a clearly understood environmental position should allow the practice to take a leading role in the future of sustainable architecture and urbanism in this country.

2

1 Window installation, Selfridges & Co, London

2 The Springseat, product (collaboration with Nicholas Mival)

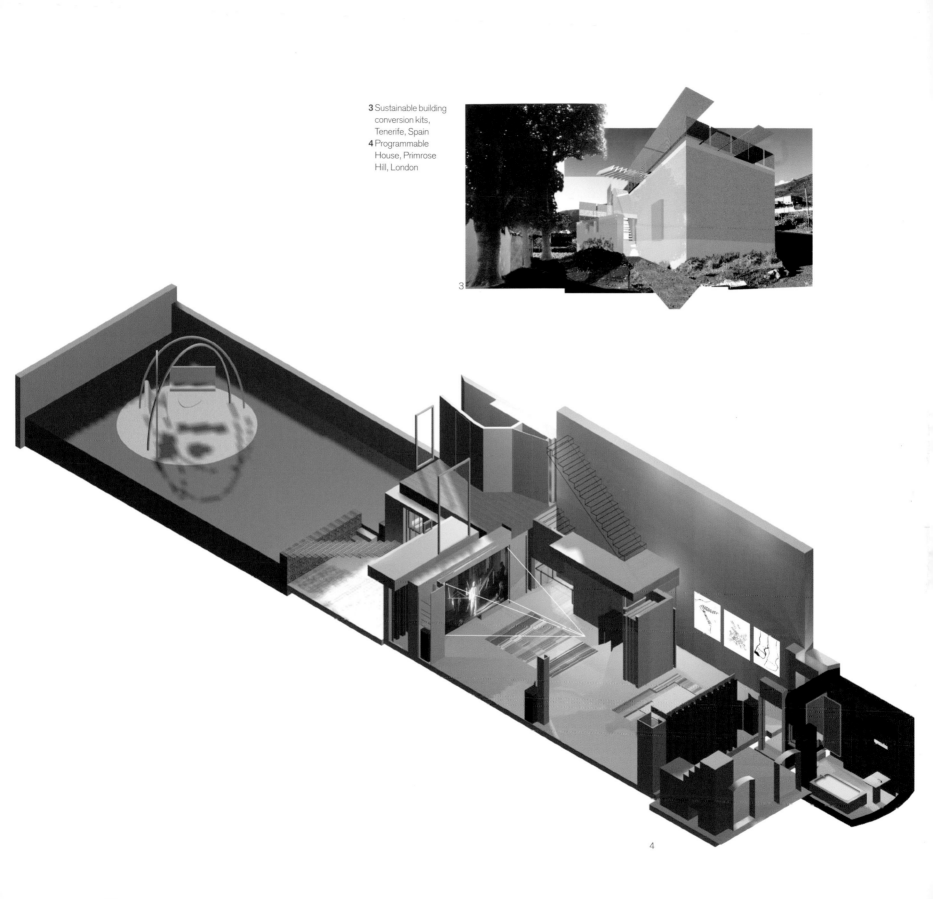

3 Sustainable building
 conversion kits,
 Tenerife, Spain
4 Programmable
 House, Primrose
 Hill, London

3

4

David Mikhail Architects
173 Upper Street
London N1 1RG
T   020 7704 8318
F   020 7226 8324
E   david@dmikhail.freeserve.co.uk

David Mikhail Architects

In 1991, aged 28, David Mikhail's scheme won first prize for the Zagreb site in Croatia, in the Europan (2) competition, looking at housing and urban regeneration across Europe. By 1995, the practice was properly established, and current projects include largely private residential, both new-builds and refurbishments.

The regular themes of the practice's work are a "passionate enjoyment of materials" and a dedication to the principles of Modernism, with "a mistrust of 'over-design' and a desire to keep design clear and comprehensible". They "look for delight in the unexpected, drama where appropriate, coolness where not".

At present, the team is working on a new-build house for a site on a beach in Tobago in the West Indies, along with a design for a new restaurant, called Pavilion East, opposite the Imperial War Museum in Kennington, south London. The practice has recenlty completed The London Print Studio in Kensal Rise, west London.

2

1 The London Print Studio, Kensal Rise, London
2|3 Residential extension and refurbishment, Stockwell, London

1

Derek Wylie Architecture
241–251 Ferndale Road
London SW9 8BJ
T   020 7274 6373
F   020 7274 1449

Derek Wylie Architecture

The practice was established in 1996 after Wylie completed his first solo project for a restaurant in Chislehurst, Kent, and has since completed a range of projects including gallery spaces, studios, live/work spaces and residential refurbishments.

The architectural aim of the practice is to create buildings and spaces that will reflect the real needs of living and working today. This pragmatic approach demands considerable intuition to prise out the primary aims of the project which, once understood, can be used to create the unexpected solutions on which this firm prides itself.

The practice is passionate about the development of construction detail and using absolutely appropriate building materials. They are keen to point to the honest use of cheap materials such as plywood, plastic sheeting and sieving mesh at the Lee House in Clerkenwell, east London, and the Clapham apartment in south London as examples of these convictions.

As sole principal, Derek Wylie leads the design but is obviously keen to encourage his two young assistants to participate in the process.

The team's largest project to date was for a dance group that wanted to improve its facilities in the borough halls, which were rented from Greenwich Council. This has developed into a £7m refurbishment, restoration and conversion involving English Heritage and a private developer.

This is an innovative and exciting proposal, with an interesting use of space to 'merge' uses – dance theatre, restaurants, workshops, studios and offices – while retaining the listed structure.

The team won an RIBA award in 1997 for the conversion of a house and silversmith workshop in Clerkenwell, east London. It is a delightful and imaginative use of an old workshop behind the original Georgian houses and shops. It shows as much delight in detail as in achieving an innovative plan.

1 Disabled artist's studio, Finchley, London
2 Lee residence, Clerkenwell, London

3 Residential refurbishment, Clapham, London
4 Multi-media gallery space, King's Cross, London

DIVE Architects
10 Park Street
London SE1 9AB
T   020 7407 0955
E   dive.ia@virgin.net

DIVE Architects

This English-Swedish collaboration was founded in 1997. As most of its projects are residential at the moment, its focus is to give the client the best space possible, creating light and connecting the design to its surrounding environment.

Recurring themes in its work are the formation of physical planes, depth and opacity; material quality and colour in turn become integral to the space. The architecture bases itself on creating a balance between practicality and aesthetic impact.

As a small firm, it values creative input from other design disciplines and it shares office space with photographers, graphic designers, textile designers and painters. Other projects include a design for a chiropodist's surgery, a restaurant, and several exhibitions at the Royal College of Art.

DIVE's two partners have backgrounds in office work, one at Blauel Architects and the other at Harper McKay, but most of the practice's work so far has been residential and very small scale. Its most significant project so far is its 'glass house' loft fit-out for two artists in London.

The main move was to place colourful pods along the centre of the space, dividing it into two and providing space for the inhabitants to live and to hang an extensive collection of contemporary art. Neat ideas such as a huge light-box on one wall create a place of real character, and the use of colour is a pleasure – DIVE is not doing conventional minimal interiors.

The use of colour is perhaps the most distinctive element of DIVE's work. This comes to the fore in its small office fit-out for a children's publishing house. This is a small project, but it is bold and colourful, reflecting the brand values of the client and providing an attractive reception space. DIVE clearly has concerns beyond residential interiors – competition entries show strong environmental concerns – and it awaits opportunities to explore them.

1

1|2 The Glass House,
   residential
   refurbishment,
   Bermondsey,
   London

2

3|4 Residential conversion, Bankside, London

DRDH Architects
Unit 1/2
47-49 Tudor Road
London E9 7SN
T 020 8510 0550
F 020 8510 0550
E drdh.a@virgin.net

DRDH Architects

DRDH has worked on projects of varying scales, from furniture and lighting design to commercial architecture, civic spaces and buildings.

The practice aims "to engage with contemporary issues of culture and inhabitation, through rigorous interrogation and a belief in design as a means of addressing both the spatial and the programatic within a wider social and economic context". This translates into a special interest in live/work spaces which can embrace all the aspects of contemporary living, including the changing shape of the family and the necessity of flexible working space and hours. The partners are also concerned that their architecture, however small the project, makes a positive contribution to its environment.

A relatively young practice with a growing client base in the north of England, in particular Sheffield and Leeds, as well as London. It specializes in working with people with a creative background, such as those in advertising, artists and gallery owners. As a consequence, several of its projects have included live/work spaces with galleries and studios. Other work includes urban regeneration projects and the team has acted as design consultants in both Sheffield and Leeds.

The practice is commercially astute and highly regarded by housing developers for its innovative planning.

1 Residential conversion, Islington, London
2|3 Bar, Showroom, Sheffield

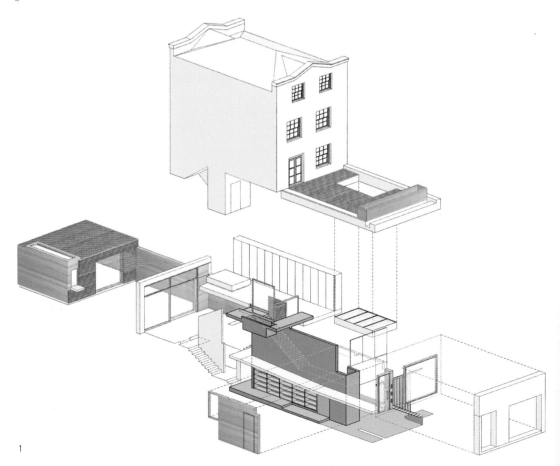

1

3

4 Rooftop gallery and
residential conversion,
Hoxton, London
5 Offices,
Iris Associates,
Sheffield

5

DSDHA
76 Loughborough Road
London SW9 7SB
T   020 7501 9299
F   020 7703 3890
E   dsdha@lineone.net

DSDHA

Formed in 1998 by Deborah Saunt and David Hills, this practice has wide-ranging experience that includes conservation work with listed buildings, collaboration with artists, re-branding and retail identity as well as large-scale urban regeneration proposals. The partners understand architecture and design in terms of the tensions that modern life creates.

Their aim is to negotiate between diverse and often contradictory interests in order to find new solutions, whether on the scale of mass housing and new city conditions or on the scale of an early project, Divorced House, for a divorced couple and their children. It is important to them to be able to provide a 'both-and' instead of an 'either-or' solution. While they use the latest technologies, they are not pre-occupied with quick fix solutions or fashion statements and simply want to create an intelligent response to any architectural challenge.

This innovative practice sets out to challenge preconceptions about architecture.

DSDHA sees its role as negotiating between the city and the individual. It sees architects as the catalyst for urban regeneration and understands the economics of producing 'good' architecture.

DSDHA are able to generate popular interest in architecture.

2

1 Plovers Hill
Orangery, Norfolk
2 Hospice,
north London
3 Hairdresser, ZOO,
Islington, London

1

East Architects
90 Queensland Road
London N7 7AS
T   020 7609 0444
F   020 7609 9844
E   mail@east-london.demon.co.uk

East Architects

East is a north-London-based urban strategy, architecture and landscape practice that concentrates on projects of public relevance. The firm's work is recognized for its provocative role in urban regeneration, and it has attracted a great deal of attention for its sensitive environmental improvements for councils along the recent London Underground's Jubilee Line Extension project. The practice is unusually small, in an area of architecture that has been dominated by a handful of what it calls "solid, frequently stolid, heavyweight consultancies", but its projects are increasing in size and are often high-profile.

The second phase of its improvements to Borough High Street, south London, will be completed this year.

East is also leading the urban design and landscape aspects of Arsenal Football Club's proposal for a new sixty-thousand-seat stadium in north London, as well as being instrumental in the development of other sites in the area, such as Islington Council's main depot, workshop and waste-transfer facilities.

1 Signage, Southwark, London
2 Winning proposal for Car-Free London initiative, The Architecture Foundation, London

3-6 Street improvements, Borough, London

3

4

5

6

Eldridge Smerin
17 Cinnamon Row
Plantation Wharf
London SW11 3TW
T 020 7228 2824
F 020 7228 2825
E mail@eldridgesmerin.com

Eldridge Smerin

Nick Eldridge and Piers Smerin formed this practice in 1998 with a wealth of experience in established architectural practices. Nick Eldridge was formerly an associate of Foster and Partners, director of Troughton McAslan and design director of John McAslan and Partners. Smerin worked for Zaha Hadid, Foster and Partners and Simon Conder before joining McAslan.

Together they are developing a wide-ranging portfolio, including housing and living environments, a restaurant and a fit-out of the London headquarters of an international sports media group.

The practice has recently been commissioned to create a state-of-the-art research facility for a division of British Telecom. Most of its experience is residential, and it has aimed to adapt and invigorate existing environments with high-quality contemporary interventions.

Eldridge Smerin tries to "challenge conventional ideas on how new ways of living can be introduced into an established urban order to produce drama and delight".

The buildings are adapted to work well for the people who use them. Both partners work closely with clients and enjoy creating entire environments. Ideas are communicated using drawings, models, visualizations and plans. Technology is used where appropriate for projects.

This practice seeks to create the best from existing structures. It sees architecture as bringing sculptural as well as spatial qualities to the space, and its goal is to provide classic rather than fashionable solutions.

1 Office conversion,
Centre Point,
London
2 Residential
conversion, Pimlico,
London

2

3

3|4 Residential
new-build, Highgate,
London

1

Evans Vettori Architects
The Old Butchers
76 Rutland Road
Matlock
Derbyshire DE4 3GN
T 01629 760559
F 01629 760560
E mail@vettori.co.uk

Evans Vettori Architects

The practice's work ranges from small domestic projects, buildings for both the primary and higher education sectors, religious and community buildings and, most recently, an industrial scheme for play-equipment manufacturers, in collaboration with Arup.

Early work includes inserting new bedrooms into a chapel in Cornwall, producing more accommodation within the existing volume.

Robert Evans, the principal, teaches at Sheffield University School of Architecture and believes the connection between practice and teaching is important in retaining a critical edge.

The practice was set up in 1995, and projects, which range in budget from £50,000 to £1.4m, show a steady increase in size and control. A sensitive and clear response to context characterises Evans Vettori's work.

The largest completed project to date, the Nottingham Trent University School of Art and Design building in Nottingham, is an intervention between an existing Italianate and post-war functionalist pair of buildings. A reconfiguring of the space between the two structures to produce a resonance between them increased the usability of the building and incorporated intelligent and well-crafted interventions and details.

Recent schemes include converting derelict barns in central Lancashire into housing. These are definitely not 'barn conversions', and they develop themes of working in a rural situation from a rigorous analysis of context.

1

1|2 School of Art &
Design, Nottingham
Trent University,
Nottingham

2

3 Residential
  extension, Cornwall
4 Refurbishment,
  Newlyn Art Gallery,
  Cornwall

Format Milton Architects
Format House
17–19 High Street
Alton
Hampshire GU34 1AW
T   01420 82131
F   01420 83400
E   mail@formatmilton.co.uk

Format Milton Architects

This practice was formed in the early 1990s, and one of its first projects – a regenerative housing project in Tampere, Finland – was a winning entry in Europan 4 (1996). Since its early residential work, the practice has added education and community projects to its list of award-winning projects. Now that project size is increasing, Format Milton is tackling specialist health-related projects, interior design and urban planning.

The practice enjoys using environmental technology which allows it to reduce cost-in-use. Communication technology is also used to good effect within the design teams by posting project drawings for shared use on a secure website. Whilst the practice pursues a Modernist solution for all its work, it is now finding considerable success converting historic buildings. Current projects include the conversion of a 3000 sq m maltings building, dating from 1850, to a community facility in Hampshire.

The practice philosophy of integrating environmental aspects and structural solutions to generate contemporary architecture is evident in its work. In the Pokesdown School project in Bournemouth, for example, 'lightscoops' bring natural ventilation and light into the heart of the building.

Sensitive detailing, coupled with dramatic structural solutions, is demonstrated in work at Alton College, Hampshire, and at the house in Camberley, Surrey. Larger projects, such as the proposals for new housing at Tampere in Finland, show great originality. A mix of UK terraced housing and open European courtyards create an innovative, high-density project.

2

1

1 Pokesdown
   Primary School,
   Bournemouth
2 Conversion and
   new-build offices
   and shops, Alton,
   Hampshire

3|4 Residential new-
build, Camberley,
Surrey

Gareth Hoskins Architects
Atlantic Chambers
45 Hope Street
Glasgow G2 6AE
T   0141 564 1255
F   0141 564 1451
E   hoskinsarchitect@zoom.co.uk

Gareth Hoskins Architects

The practice, set up by Gareth Hoskins in 1998, has so far won several competitions for prominent projects, such as the Mackintosh Centre in Glasgow, Scotland, as well as smaller projects for private houses.

In its housing schemes, GHA explores ideas of living within urban and rural environments and has developed social projects that tackle issues of homelessness and healthcare.

The practice has just been appointed to design experimental housing for young homeless people and recently completed the redesign of care environments for people with dementia.

Members of the practice remain closely involved in architectural teaching through their roles as visiting critics and lecturers at a number of schools.

People and how they encounter place and space are at the heart of the practice's approach. This is evident in work at the acclaimed Mackintosh Centre, Glasgow, and at the meeting room of the Saughlan Prison Visitors Centre, Edinburgh.

This ethos is informed by the work of Mexican architect Luis Barragán and his celebration of magic and delight combined with intimacy and silence.

1 Charles Rennie MacKintosh interpretation centre, Lighthouse, Glasgow

2 Cor-ten steel display, Durham Light Infantry Museum, Durham

3|4 Saughton Prison Visitors Centre, HM Prison, Edinburgh

Glas Architects and Designers
Unit 4
51 Tanner Street
London SE1 3PL
T   020 7378 7755
F   020 7378 7722
E   mail@glas.ltd.uk

Glas Architects and Designers

Stas Louca and Nazar Sayigh formed Glas in 1998, and in the past twenty-four months Glas has planned and constructed eighteen projects that include commercial and industrial units, new and refurbished residential, and sports facilities. The practice recently won its first competition, for Tower House School's new hall in Sheen, south west London.

The starting point for all the practice's projects is the idea that function gives shape to form and space. The practice "prioritizes attention to detail and is committed to innovation, seeking original uses for traditional and modern materials'.

Glas are an impressive outfit. The partners are only thirty-one years old, but they have already built three relatively major office buildings and are working on a host of smaller private schemes. The firm has also recently broken into the education sector, with a scheme for a new music suite and school hall.

Glas is also a practice that sees itself as part of the construction industry, which is refreshing. It is interested in the Egan agenda and has used an impressive degree of prefabrication in its projects, particularly on an office project in Southwark, south London, where panels of multi-coloured resins are incorporated into the facade.

Perhaps the most exciting project is the new school building in Tower Hill, south west London, which is an ingenious plan with a hall at the centre of three new rooms. This scheme provides many facilities for the £400,000 budget.

2

1 Residential conversion, Tyers Gate, London
2 Residential refurbishment, Notting Hill, London

1

3|4 Offices, Fellmongers
Path, London

Gregory Phillips Architects
66 Great Cumberland Place
London W1H 7FD
T   020 7724 3040
F   020 7724 3020
E   gpa@gregoryphillips.com

Gregory Phillips Architects

The practice, established in 1991 by Gregory Phillips, has evolved so that all office members now provide skilled input into each project and the practice's organisational systems.

The practice does not intend to impose solutions on its clients, but works with them to create results that answer the issues at the heart of the brief. Gregory Phillips Architects is committed to working with the skills and crafts that are available to produce solutions that work and look elegant. The way junctions are formed, the choice of materials and the manipulation of space and light are dominant concerns.

It has worked on projects of varying scale, from a new-build £7m hotel in London, due for completion in 2002, to twenty coffee bars for Coffee Republic, for which each location's design could be constructed within three weeks.

This highly competent practice aims to combine design ability with professionalism to deliver solutions that exceed client expectations. Working with the ethos "think like them, then think for them", much of the current work is repeat commissions.

A broad spread of work includes a number of interiors, as well as buildings involving complex planning issues. Innovative projects are not necessarily high-tech but use traditional materials in new ways. This is described as "modern/traditional".

Careful detailing encourages a high level of craftsmanship. Construction is generally rugged and designed to last, and sustainability issues underpin designs where possible.

2

1 Office conversion,
  Soho, London
2 Residential
  new-build, St John's
  Wood, London

1

3|4 New-build housing
scheme, Ballinrobe,
Co.Mayo, Ireland
5|6 New-build hotel
propsal, Regent's
Park, London

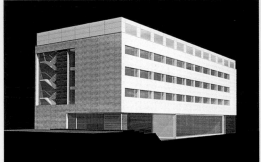
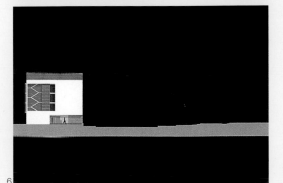

Houlton Taylor Architects
133 Curtain Rd
London EC2A 3BX
T   020 7729 1451
F   020 7729 1525
E   architects@houltontaylor.demon.co.uk

Andrew Houlton and Stephen Taylor formed this practice in 1994. Since then, it has worked on a range of projects, including a mausoleum, a theatre, a student hostel, doctors' surgeries, and residential units for a special needs school in Cumbria. Current projects include a nursery school for the West London Synagogue.

The practice recently contributed to an exhibition entitled, 'Encounters'. Here they presented an outline of their approach, which "places an emphasis upon the moment in which to decipher an appropriate exchange", providing the point of departure that often leads towards their design for a commission.

Houlton Taylor's work is essentially confident yet understated, with a concern for maximizing value with often taxing budgets.

The architects, whose partners also teach at the Architectural Association, describe their work as an "assimilation of the things we find". They show a concern for sustainability, enjoy materials and problem-solving, and boast a happy relationship with clients.

Houlton Taylor's projects are all assured, serious, with an affinity for glass and 'clean' lines.

1 Extension, Derwent Medical Centre, Harrow, London
2-4 New-build, Children's Home, Riverside School, Cumbria

Jamie Fobert Architects
5 Crescent Row
London EC1Y OSP
T 020 7553 6560
F 020 7553 6566
E jfa-@dircon.co.uk

Jamie Fobert Architects

Finding the 'subject of the work' and understanding what its role is within the finished project is central to this practice's approach.

The 'subject of the work' is not necessarily the building's use, but could be "something else; the tranquil room, the changing sky, solidity and weight. A tone not described by words".

Recent work includes a restaurant, bar and music venue in Shoreditch, east London, and an addition to an Arts and Crafts house in Hampstead, north-west London, both of which were completed in 2000.

Aveda, the American natural cosmetics company, approached the practice to develop a design strategy for its new stores in 1998. The first store was built in Marylebone High Street in central London, and a second has recently been completed in Notting Hill, west London. Further stores will be built in Glasgow, Scotland, and Covent Garden, central London.

Jamie worked with David Chipperfield and taught at the Royal College of Art before setting up his practice in 1996. He has already completed an impressive range of residential projects and retail outlets for the US cosmetics store Aveda. His work is characterized by careful attention to the choice of materials and to detailing. Natural timber, raw concrete and waxed steel all feature regularly in his vocabulary. The focus is on honesty to the nature of the materials used. Jamie plans to continue to give a very personal service to his clients, from design to delivery.

1 Office Foyer, James Street, London
2 Cargo bar, Rivington Street, London
3 Grosz Residence, Hampstead, London

4 Dwek residence,
  Belsize Park, London
5 Shop, Aveda Institute,
  Westbourne Grove,
  London
6 Cafe, Aveda Institute,
  Marylebone, London

John Pardey Architect
Eastwood Studio
Ridgeway Lane
Lymington
Hampshire SO41 8AA
T 01590 677226
F 01590 677226
E pardey.arch@virgin.net

John Pardey has won many awards for his residential work, which is based on a close dialogue with each client to ensure that the brief is both met and brought to a higher plane. He specializes in one-off, high-quality projects, and his ideal is to create a timelessness in each work as well as a delight in the ordinary. He avoids waste and strives to an efficient use of energy and resources, but does not base his designs on such issues alone. Pardey prides himself on his ability to work to deadlines and to budget while ensuring he gives the personal service he believes is missing in many of the larger commercial practices. His work has featured in a number of publications and has been exhibited widely.

John Pardey Architect

2

1-4 Residential refurbishment and extension, Spence House, Beaulieu, Hampshire

1

3

4

KMK Architects
W123 Westminster Business Square
Durham Street
London SE11 5HJ
T   020 7582 7527
F   020 7820 3962
E   kmk@dircon.co.uk

KMK Architects

KMK was formed in 1993 by the two partners – Mike Kane and Fawzia Muradali-Kane – following a series of small scale private commissions, carried out while the partners were working in separate architectural practices. Completed works include several private-house extensions, the refurbishment of a night hostel for the homeless in Soho, central London, and new-build residential accommodation for special-needs clients such as long-term alcohol abusers and victims of domestic violence. Their projects have been published in *The Architects' Journal, The Guardian*, *The Independent* and various fashion magazines. The apartments they have designed at Baltic Street and Peartree Street in east London are regularly used as locations for fashion shoots, movies and pop videos.

KMK has produced a number of very professional and 'good-looking' residential projects for developers and private clients. These all show an enthusiasm for glass and other slick materials.

The practice's two most important projects so far are both residential. One is a private house refurbishment in Limehouse, east London, which backs on to the river Thames. A slick glass wall at the back provides amazing views of the river. A mix of materials inside the Grade II listed house divides the building into private house and semi-private office space for the owner.

1 Residential refurbishment, Limehouse, London
2 Residential and office space, Clerkenwell, London
3 Residential and offices, King's Cross, London
4 Residential conversion, Clerkenwell, London

Knott Architects

Knott Architects
98b Tollington Park
London N4 3RB
T   020 7263 8844
F   020 7263 8844
E   mail@knottarchitects.co.uk

This design-led practice was formed by brothers George and Tom Knott in 1994. They believe that good design improves the quality of life. The work that results from this belief is a crafted Modernism that respects each situation as unique.

Members of the practice bring with them experience of a variety of projects in major developments, including business parks, hotels, restaurants, bars and public buildings. The firm has completed a number of residential projects as well as high-profile retail outlets for the Karen Millen fashion outlet on Brompton Road and Kensington High Street, both in west London.

Current work includes offices in the Brunswick Centre, central London, and competition entries for a bus station, a marine centre and a series of art galleries in Norway.

1|2|4 Residential and studio space, London

3 Residential conversion, Bankside, London

Letts Wheeler Architecture and Design
Studio 10, Ayr Street Workshops
Ayr Street
Nottingham NG7 4FX
T   0115 911 0734
F   0115 911 0734
E   lettswheeler@innotts.co.uk

Letts Wheeler

The practice was formed in 1996, and has carried out a wide variety of projects, ranging from a silversmith's studio to sheltered housing. Clients include Nottingham Trent University, the Earth Centre in Rotherham, housing associations and private developers. Although the projects are small, their potential to change the nature of their immediate spatial and social context is a primary concern. The two sites at Nottingham Trent University, for instance, originally faced onto a neglected space on the campus. The movement and interaction that have been created by the new buildings have allowed the courtyard created between them to become a viable public space. Over the past year the scale of projects has increased, and the firm is currently working on The Nottingham High School for Boys, and a recording studio.

In the architectural desert of the East Midlands, Letts Wheeler's practice sits like an oasis. Their work is informed by sound pragmatic principles where a 'minimalist' architecture consistently emerges free from stylistic mannerism. This is reinforced by an architectural language derived from a very limited palette of materials. Letts Wheeler's work is 'project-specific' rather than 'generic'. Built work has characteristically been subject to severe constraints, be they generated by site, client's brief or cost. It is the imaginative response to such constraints that makes their work so distinctive and refreshing – a 'serendipity' which allows for the unpredicted and unrehearsed to happen. With a £1m project on site and a £3.5m project submitted for planning approval, the future of Letts Wheeler looks bright.

1 Residential new-build, near Petworth, West Sussex
2 Residential extension, Nottingham
3|4 Nature Works Pavilion at The Earth Centre, Rotherham, South Yorkshire
5 Globar, The Students' Union, Nottingham Trent University, Nottingham (in association with Wolfgang and Heron)

Loates-Taylor Shannon
Architects and Designers
11–12 Great Sutton Street
London EC1V 0BX
T   020 7689 0070
E   lts@btinternet.com
W   www.lts-architects.co.uk

Loates-Taylor Shannon

Michael Loates-Taylor and Greg Shannon formed LTS in 1996, and have since built up a client list that includes Haringey and Oxfordshire City Councils, Regalian Properties, Cadogan Estates and Guardian Royal Exchange. The practice has recently completed the conversion of a Grade II listed wharf building into thirty-eight apartments, and has another four comparable new-build projects at the planning stage. On a smaller scale, the firm has three new-build modern houses on site across London and has completed three new-media office environments, one incorporating an interactive marketing research facility. The practice tries to maintain an open and responsive approach to design problems, and is motivated by creating environments that support and enhance people's lives.

Both partners originally trained as interior designers before retraining as architects. This background has informed their design approach and was originally the source of their client base. LTS Architects' work has a calm, rational approach, creating flexible spaces with considerable use of glass for both walls and floors. It has a strong interest in light and lighting, manipulating daylight and creating 'washes' of colour through use of neon. Efficient planning and careful detailing has led to repeat work from housing developers and a growing workload in this area. In addition, the firm works in the fields of mixed-use and light industrial buildings. It is gradually moving into education, health and recreation buildings and has formed Framework, a company offering an innovative approach to pre-engineered volumetric buildings. Its work is considered and sensitive, and it analyzes each project to produce appropriate and innovative solutions.

1|5 Hairdressers,
Wimbledon, London
2 Residential
refurbishment,
Limehouse, London

3 Residential and office space, The Listed Building, Free Trade Wharf, London

4 Ticket booth competition, Times Square, New York

Loyn and Co. Architects
Penarth
Vale of Glamorgan, Wales
CF64 3EG
T 029 2071 1432
F 029 2040 2784
E chris.loyn@virgin.net

Loyn & Co. Architects

Established in 1992, the practice's work ranges from sensitive refurbishment, including work with listed structures, through to the creation of contemporary new buildings. Experience includes one-off residential projects, multiple housing/apartment complexes and commercial premises, as well as interior design, fit-out and space planning.

In addition to mainstream architecture, Loyn & Co. has also undertaken commissions for furniture design and offer an in-house illustration service, preparing perspectives for other companies.

The size of the practice varies between three and six people according to workload. Founder Chris Loyn is involved with the Welsh School of Architecture and the University of Wales Institure.

Loyn & Co. is passionate about contemporary design and this is evident in its projects. Initial meetings with clients involve a series of sketches and watercolours, all in three dimensions.

A passion for detail is also apparent in the projects. Context is very important and influences all designs, and sustainability is becoming a key issue.

Loyn & Co. obviously cares about its projects and is very keen to make a positive contribution to the built environment. The firm's projects demonstrate that it is achieving this.

1 Residential
  refurbishment,
  Bradford Place,
  Bristol
2|3 Residential
  new-build, Raisdale
  Road, Penarth,
  Wales
4 Extension,
  St Donat's Art
  Centre, Wales

m3 Architects
5 Charterhouse buildings
London EC1M 7AN
T   020 7253 7255
F   020 7253 7266
E   post@m3architects.com
W   www.m3architects.com

m3 Architects

While at Foster & Partners, the founders, who formed this practice in 1997, worked on large scale projects such as the Commerzbank HQ in Frankfurt, the Millennium Tower in the City of London, the Reichstag in Berlin and Hong Kong Airport at Chep Lap Kok.

Projects at m3 range from a 92-room hotel in Stratford, east London, to a holiday home for Sir Stirling Moss. This low-energy house will feature a number of devices intended to allow the building to be controlled from anywhere in the world. It can be dismantled and relocated wherever necessary.

The practice's primary objectives include using leading edge technology to demonstrate and communicate design proposals and it believes that new buildings should, where practicable, embody the best in energy-saving and low-maintenance practice.

The energetic approach of m3 partners – Ken Hutt and Nadi Jahangiri – focuses on what design can do for either the client or the site. This is then executed in a clear and modern style.

Its residential projects demonstrate its use of design as an agent for lifestyle change. The same approach can be seen in what it describes as its "project making" endeavours. For example, its 108-storey 'eco-tower' (site to be determined) or its unsolicited proposal to redevelop the forecourt of King's Cross Station in central London. Clearly an ambitious and capable oufit.

1 Citygate Eco-tower
   proposal, London
2 Residential conversion,
   Clerkenwell,
   London

3 Residential
extension, Epping
Forest, Essex
4 Canary riverside
competition, Canary
Wharf, London

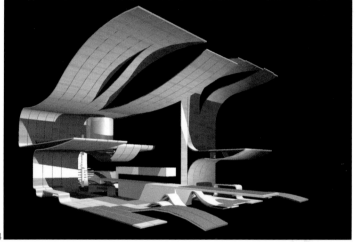

4

3

Magyar Marsoni Architects
18 Avonmore Road
London W14 8RR
T   020 7603 8800
F   020 7603 8868
E   studio@mmarchitects.co.uk

Magyar Marsoni Architects

Magyar Marsoni Architects was founded in 1999 by architects wanting to move away from more cumbersome and traditional models of architectural practice. One of its main objectives was to pursue new ways of thinking about design problems, from a broad cultural and historical base without losing sight of a client's pragmatic and commercial requirements.

Its projects have included masterplanning office, leisure and retail space in Canary Wharf in east London's docklands, the design and completion of corporate headquarters in Budapest, a family house in northern Italy and workplace interiors in London. It is currently working on a project of five railway stations for Connex Trains in south-east England.

A strong practice with two principals – both from major commercial practice, Fitzroy Robinson – with extensive experience in work with a strong design ethos.

The practice started with office fit-outs and from 2000 was dealing with schemes of up to 4000 sq m. It has two major office projects in Budapest, Hungary, of 3500 sq m. The firm is very 'marketing-minded' and has an innovative design culture, with 'design' partners producing concepts. It is affiliated to 4UM Group, providing greater resource for large-scale projects.

1 Office refurbishment, Battersea, London
2|4 Residential refurbishment and new-build, Biela, Italy
3 Offices, new-build, Budapest, Hungary

McDaniel Woolf
Larkfield Studios
32 Larkfield Road
Richmond
Surrey TW9 2PF
T   020 8332 1981
F   020 8332 9094
E   richard@mcdanielwoolf.co.uk

McDaniel Woolf

This is a multi-disciplined architectural and design practice, established in 1995 by Fiona McDaniel and Richard Woolf. Early projects were predominantly interior-based with low budgets, requiring the innovative use of simple materials. This approach remains the cornerstone of the practice's design methodology.

Perhaps the practice's best-known work is for Japanese retailer Muji, for whom it designed a series of ten stores, including those on Tottenham Court Road and Long Acre, both in central London.

Its interest in design and culture is not limited to the built environment but also embraces furniture and product design.

Richard Woolf is sole active principal leading a staff of seven, plus two freelancers. Woolf, who trained originally as an industrial designer, has broad experience from previous stints with Harper Mackay, Fitch & Company and SBT. Commissions are, in the main, repeat business or recommendations.

Current major projects include a £1.6m extension to the Richmond Brewery Stores building in south-west London, providing new office and studio accommodation within a conservation area, and a £600,000 office scheme at Farnborough, Hampshire.

The office is well-organised and dedicated to a hands-on approach. The practice has undertaken almost one hundred architectural, interior, furniture and product design commissions.

2

3

1 Percival David
  Foundation,
  School of Oriental
  and African Studies,
  London
2 Offices, Hilson
  Moran, Farnborough

3|4 Muji, Tottenham
    Court Road, London

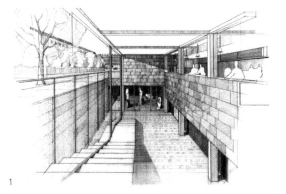

1

McKeown Alexander Architects
14 King Street
Glasgow G1 5QP
T   0141 572 2011
F   0141 572 2012
E   studio@mcka.demon.co.uk

McKeown Alexander Architects

McKeown Alexander is an experienced practice with a keen theoretical edge. Work (mostly in Glasgow or Paisley, and mostly residential) includes twenty flats in Graham Square, a fifteen-flat scheme in the 'Homes for the Future' site at Glasgow Green and a modest office scheme in Kentish Town, north London.

The practice asserts that "full integration of structure, program and context, not issues of architectural style, provide the core architectural ingredients of good design".

It is also committed to energy-efficient design that maximizes free-energy gains and minimizes energy-loss. The approach to sustainable design not only considers the specification of materials from renewable sources but also the adaptability of a project for its constantly evolving uses.

Current projects include twenty flats to the value of £1m, a set of studios and a restaurant on the banks of the River Clyde in Glasgow, worth £1m, several fit-outs and a new-build private house.

The practice's mission is pragmatic and progressive – a realistic desire to bring projects in on time and on budget is always infused with imagination.

Underlying the apparent instrumentalism is a research approach. The practice has an extensive architectural literature and established figures like Kahn, Breuer and Zumthor are referenced besides newcomers like Herzog and de Meuron. Teaching is seen as important as a way of continually re-animating this practice.

2

1

1|4 New-build
    residential, Homes
    for the Future,
    Glasgow
  2 Residential
    refurbishment,
    Jaspan House,
    Glasgow

3 Residential
new-build, Graham
Square, Glasgow

3

4

muf architecture/art
49–51 Central Street
London EC1V 8AB
T   020 7251 4004
F   020 7250 1967
E   studio@muf.co.uk

muf architecture/art

This practice is a collaboration
of artists and architects that is
committed to working in the public
realm. It was formed in 1994,
by artist Katherine Clarke and
architects Juliet Bidgood and
Liza Fior. Since then, the team
has been joined by three more
architects and another artist.

The work addresses both the
physical and the social fabric of
the urban environment, and it
aims to increase enjoyment and
appreciation of public spaces
by "making room for speculative
dreaming and imaginative thinking".

The practice's process of design
development encouranges an
understanding of the views, desires
and skills of those people that live,
work or play in an area, and the
team constantly seeks effective
means of consultation, negotiation
and collaboration to achieve
appropriate solutions.

Recent projects include the
£1.2m scheme of environmental
improvements called 'Shared
Ground', which forms part of
Southwark Council's widespread
regeneration program in
south London.

3

1|2 Installation,
shop-window, Ocean
Estate, Stepney,
London
3 Street improvements,
Stoke-on-Trent
City Centre

1

2

4 Street improvements, Southwark, London

5 Installation, 'Associate – Love at First Sight Living Room', Walsall Festival, Walsall

6 Design for BMX bike track, Salt Mills Millennium Park, Saltash, Cornwall

Oliver Chapman Architects
9/1 Brougham Street
Edinburgh EH3 9JS
T   0131 229 7655
F   0131 229 7655
E   oliver@ocarchitects.freeserve.co.uk

Oliver Chapman Architects

Oliver Chapman set up this practice in 1997, and was runner-up in the 2000 Young Architect of the Year competition.

The themes he recognizes in his work include an interest in form over context, and in surprise and fun. His approach to domestic architecture centres on refining a dialogue with a client to personalize domestic space. He also tries to find spatial devices that add to the layers of privacy in a home, such as the interlocking volumes in a design for an interior called 'Bed Box'.

A current proposal is for a cricket pavilion that closes down seamlessly and securely when not in use, taking in all the awnings, seats, steps and scoreboard. In the event of a match taking place, all these elements open up to transform the building into a lively, active structure.

Chapman also tutors at the School of Architecture at Edinburgh University.

This is a bright, two-person practice that is about to move into new premises overlooking a street in central Edinburgh.

Its designs are carefully crafted with a fondness for beautiful timberwork. It explores changing volumes, planes and levels and their effects on perception. The practice shows a particular interest in the public-versus-the-private domain and in unlocking opportunities from 'boxes within boxes'.

Oliver Chapman Architects also covers exhibition design and has an interest in ventilation and ecological design. The practice has completed work throughout the UK.

2

3

1

1|3 Residential
    refurbishment,
    Edinburgh New
    Town, Scotland
  2 Residential interior,
    'Bed Box',
    Edinburgh, Scotland
  4 Residential
    refurbishment,
    Edinburgh, Scotland

Peter Meacock Central Workshop
2 All Saints Court
Bristol BS1 1JN
T 01179 257077
F 01179 250078
E centralworkshop@cablenet.co.uk

Peter Meacock Central Workshop

Current work includes two villas in Somerset, a historical museum for Antwerp, a number of residential refurbishments, new-build apartments, temporary structures for an International Festival of the Sea and the Southville Arts and Community Centre in Bristol.

The practice recently completed the Severnshed Restaurant on Bristol's dockside, and generated a great deal of attention from both general and trade media. The building was originally designed by Brunel as a demountable shed, and is the last surviving example of the nine that were built in the 1800s. Peter Meacock, in collaboration with Matthew Pruen and Kevin Wright, designed a seven-metre-long stainless steel 'Hoverbar' that is moved around the space through the use of four hover pads, filled with compressed air. The practice is committed to producing buildings that are genuinely environmentally responsible.

The practice is buried in a courtyard just yards from the central financial district of Bristol. At present, the early nineteenth-century terrace house that is home to the office is in the throes of a major makeover.

Well-equipped, with a battery of Apple computers, physical models evidently play a large part in design development. Although there are two completed buildings with a major public presence in the centre of Bristol, all the work is for private clients.

The projects vary in scale from a successful, but awkward, grain loft-to-apartment conversion to an ingenious fit-out of a slide library.

The finished projects exhibit a concern for careful specification of material and a determined demand for a high quality of finish.

The practice's work is characterized by an innovative and radical use of technology.

1 Slide library, University of Bristol
2 Matthew Visitors Centre, Redcliffe Wharf, Bristol
3|4 Severnshed restaurant with Hoverbar, Bristol

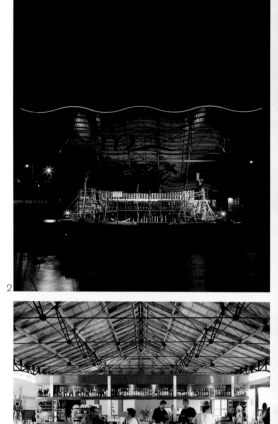

Plasma Studio
19 Meltmore Terrace
London E8 3PH
T   020 8985 5560
F   020 8985 5560
E   plasmastudio@lineone.net

Plasma Studio

Plasma Studio was formed in 1999, and since then it has pursued a design approach of project-based experimentation.

Commissions have varied from commercial to domestic, including office refurbishments, live/work accommodation and furniture design. The practice is currently working on a loft conversion and photography studio in east London, as well as two domestic refurbishments and a live/work refurbishment in Hackney, also in east London.

Plasma is seeking "an originality that introduces diversity, openness and specificity to urban planning and architecture without undermining Modernist qualities of equality, democracy and social cohesion".

Plasma partners Eva Castro and Holger Kehme have a desire to work with many disciplines – art and photography, for example – to produce their work.

Their main approach is to "reconfigure boundaries", to redefine traditional boundaries and to create new types of spatial relationships. The work produced is sculptural to look at and based on a clear rational approach.

This is a young firm of two partners, but both are ambitious and talented with a tidy and compact office set-up. The ability to produce unfamiliar and sometimes beautiful interior work on particularly low budgets is impressive.

2

1

3

1 Irish Arts and
Heritage
competition, Dublin
2|4 Retail refurbishment,
Camden, London
3 Office refurbishment,
Old Street, London

Procter:Rihl
63 Cross Street
London N1 2BB
T   020 7704 6003
F   020 7688 0478
E   info@procter-rihl.com
W   www.procter-rihl.com

Procter:Rihl

Christopher Procter and Fernando Rihl founded this practice in 1995. Since then, work has been wide-ranging and has included several domestic extensions and refurbishments, an exhibition stand for *Blueprint* magazine and a gold-medal-winning set of glass pavilions for a garden at the Chelsea Flower Show 2000 in London.

Both partners have extensive experience in environmental and energy matters: Procter has designed two solar houses in Vermont, USA, while Rihl has studied Environment and Energy, with a particular focus on daylight studies, at the Architectural Association in London.

The practice wants to challenge "the classical Modernist notion of vertical and horizontal planes" and emphasize "the ambiguity between such surfaces". Its aim is to work with local communities to develop innovative residential projects in the UK, and it believes there is a need for more cutting-edge environmentally friendly buildings, particularly housing, in this country.

1 Residential conversion, Camden, London
2 Residential loft conversion, Queen's Park, London

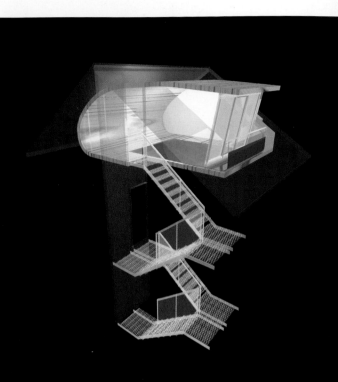

3 Residential extension and landscaping, Islington, London
4 Pavilion, Chelsea Flower Show 2000, London

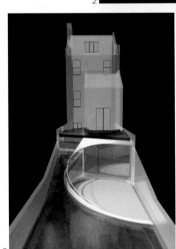

Richard Hywel Evans
14–18 Great Titchfield Street
London W1W 8BD
T   020 7436 3400
F   020 7436 3200

Richard Hywel Evans

Richard Hywel Evans worked as UK Director of Daryl Jackson International, which specializes in health and leisure, until he founded this practice. The bulk of its work has been leisure complexes, due to its wide resource of specialist knowledge. The practice has enjoyed success in both open and limited design competitions and has designed several award-winning schemes. It has also completed sports centres inside department stores such as Harrods and Selfridges, as well as an exhibition stand for Asics. The practice focuses on teamwork and involves all parties in the design process. It uses a wide variety of visual aids, including sketches, drawings and models, to encourage communication about the progression of a design, and it believes this is the only way to arrive at appropriate solutions.

Initial concepts are devised quickly by working in conjunction with the client. This shared experience culminates in an enjoyable and successful project of architectural merit. The team is influenced by the process of the automotive and marine industries and is dedicated to the enjoyment of client and project.

1 Cellular Operations
  Cafeteria, Swindon
2|3 Cellular Operations
  Headquarters,
  Swindon
4 Box Bar,
  Castlefield,
  Manchester

5 Crush juice bar,
  Clerkenwell, London
6 Emap exhibition
  stands, Interbuild
  2000

Rik Nys Design
2b Homefield Street
Hoxton
London N1 6PX
T   020 7739 8319
F   020 7684 0498
E   r.nys@unl.ac.uk

Rik Nys Design

Rik Nys Design is a young practice founded in 1998 after Nys left David Chipperfield Architects, where he was a Senior Associate. It is a design-led practice that has, so far, only completed small projects. These include several interior refurbishments and competition entries. One current project is the extension of Jenny Lo's Teahouse – a restaurant in Belgravia, central London. A large rectangular dining room will be created in the basement, and a wooden crate made of rough-cut softwood planks will be hung from the ceiling, improving acoustic conditions while forming a distinct atmosphere.

Another current project is a roof pavilion in Spitalfields, east London, where living quarters will be relocated from the top floor of a terrace to the new extension on the roof. The project will offer a sunbathing area on the back of the pavilion and a more formal terrace on the northern front.

Despite a complex and involved attitude to design, Nys's basic ethos is simple: "The only statement we, as designers, can make has to reside in the product; the final result of a process".

Rik Nys works from a studio at home. He qualified as an architect in Belgium in 1986, and is currently seeking ARB/RIBA recognition with professional indemnity. He is very professional and organized, while his work is thoughtful and considered. He enjoys working on both small highly-crafted products and objects, and on large-scale urban projects.

2

1 Ceramic jug, 'Blauw', for Slegten and Toegemann SA, Belgium
2|3 Residential refurbishment, Notting Hill, London

1

4 Residential refurbishment, Blackheath, London

4

3

Robert Dye Associates
68–74 Rochester Place
London NW1 9JX
T   020 7267 9388
F   020 7267 5963
E   rdye@btinternet.com

Robert Dye Associates

Before establishing his own practice in 1993, Robert Dye practised architecture both in the UK and abroad with James Stirling, Michael Wilford and Associates, Koetter Kim and Associates and Strand Associates. He has taught architectural design at Columbia and Washington Universities in America and urban design at the Bartlett, University of Central London.

The practice is particularly interested in developing a range of themes in its work, including the relationship between internal and external space, the continuity of horizontal and vertical surface, the definition and expansion of edges, the integration and resolution of new and old and utilizing the effects of light and colour to create bright contemporary spaces tailored to modern life. The client's brief is the starting point of the design process, rather than any preconceived ideas that the practice wishes to impose.

The office is on the brink of expansion, and current projects include a 12,000 sq m mixed-use development in Atlanta, USA, which comprises an Italian Cultural Center, retail, café and bar, studio/offices and lofts.

This practice has a team approach to projects, resulting in buildings that have their own distinct look and culture. This integrative approach also involves the client in the design process from the outset.

1 Residential conversion, Primrose Hill, London
2 Residential new-build, London
3 Conservatory, Leatherhead, Surrey

4|5 Residential
conversion,
Hampstead,
London

5

4

S333
Unit 6
246–252 St John Street
London EC1V 4PH
T 020 7490 7948
E s333arch@euronet.nl
W www.s333.org

S333

This studio for architecture and urbanism, formed in the early 1990s, has won four international housing competitions: Europan 3, Europan 4, a village extension to Vijfhuizen in The Netherlands and an urban regeneration project in Grenoble, France. In 1999, it was commended for the UK's Young Architects of the Year Award and last year it won the ABN-AMRO Award for Business Enterprise.

S333 is currently involved in a number of projects, including a mixed-use regeneration project for five hundred homes in east London, a large inner-city housing project on a six-hectare former industrial site in Groningen, The Netherlands, and the refurbishment of a castle and its grounds in Wartin, near Berlin.

It encourages new ways of thinking about, and working with, the converging relationships between architecture, urbanism and landscape.

Working as an urban consultant, S333 has been brought in by other architects such as Alsop and Stormer, as well as housing associations, to advise on urban regeneration projects. Its interest lies in acting as lead designer – it runs a unit at the Architectural Association, where it teaches 'Future practice', which examines the role the architect plays in the building process. The team redefines how architects traditionally work. Its approach to design looks at how buildings work in form and context, integrating ecology, environment and other factors.

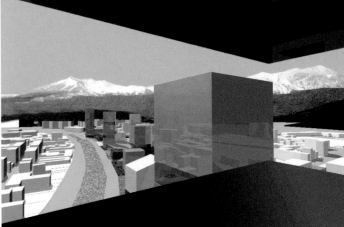

1 Dutch Mountain, Zaanstad, The Netherlands
2 Residential and retail, La Ville Foret, Grenoble, France
3 Site, Residential, Schots 1 & 2, CiBoGa Terrain, Groningen, The Netherlands

4

6

4 5 Vinex Housing,
Vijfhuizen,
The Netherlands
6 Residential, Schots
1 & 2, CiBoGa
Terrain, Groningen,
The Netherlands

5

Sarah Wigglesworth Architects
10 Stock Orchard Road
London N7 9RW
T   020 7607 9200
F   020 7607 5800
E   mail@swarch.co.uk

Sarah Wigglesworth Architects

This practice is interested in architecture that employs ordinary, readily available materials and in exploring innovative design and aesthetic strategies for sustainable building. It believes that architecture is about the construction of ideas, and its work is informed by a wide range of influences. Its most recent and best-known project is the 'Strawbale House and Quilted Office', situated in north London and completed in January 2001. A mixed-use development, the project represents a revolutionary ecological approach to design in an urban environment. The buildings use a series of experimental technologies, researched and developed especially for the project, that have a wider application for mass-production. The practice has designed cultural buildings, offices, private houses and structures for education, arts and sport. Its work has been published extensively in all media and has been featured in numerous exhibitions.

1 Yorkshire Gateways Competition, design for acoustic barriers to motorways, Yorkshire
2 New-build, writer's cabin, Highgate, London

3|4 'The Strawbale House and Quilted Office', office and residential new-build, Holloway, London

Satellite Design Workshop
30 Harcourt Street
London W1H 4HT
T   020 7723 2292
F   020 7723 6622
E   info.satellite@virgin.net

Satellite Design Workshop

This practice was formed in 1995 by Stewart Dodd and Neil Wilson. Its vision is to engage in and foster the cross-fertilization of ideas between all the creative professions.

Although its initial workload was based on small residential and commercial projects, the firm is now beginning to explore new and diverse areas, with a growing number of collaborators. It enjoys the excitement and challenge of working with artists, choreographers and film makers outside the normal parameters of architecture.

The work currently includes competition work involving urban strategies, new-build commercial projects, refurbishment projects, small-scale retail work and restaurants. One of the largest projects to date is a £1.4m office building in Kings Cross, central London. The directors are also involved in research and teaching.

This highly professional office already has a fine record in repeat clients and a strong reputation for excellent relations with contractors. Contracts normally come in on time and on budget, and are well-managed. The practice is competent at determining and addressing client needs, and details and material are carefully considered. Design information is communicated effectively to clients using sketches and models. This is a responsible practice offering an excellent service on all fronts.

1 Refurbishment,
  The Actors' Centre,
  Covent Garden,
  London
2 Installation, Shelf
  Life, South East
  Dance Agency

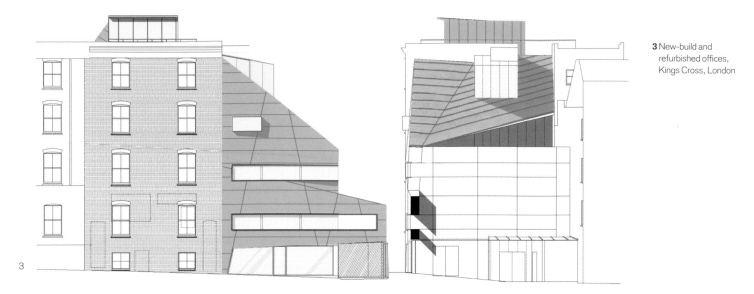

3 New-build and refurbished offices, Kings Cross, London

4 Residential extension, Notting Hill, London

5 Residential refurbishment, Ladbroke Grove, London

Softroom

Softroom
34 Lexington Street
London W1F OLH
T 020 7437 1550
F 020 7437 1566
E softroom@softroom.com

Softroom was founded in 1995, by Christopher Bagot, Dan Evans and Oliver Salway. In addition to a growing portfolio of original built projects, Softroom seeks to promote the relevance of architecture to other cultural spheres. It's recently completed shelter for walkers in Northumbria won a RIBA Award for Architecture, a Stephen Lawrence Prize and a Royal Fine Arts Commission Trust 'Building of the Year 2000' Award. The shelter doubles as a waiting point for the local ferry, and is helping to generate sustainable tourism in a remote area.

Current projects include live/work units at Tower Bridge in south London, the menswear departments of Selfridges & Co. and a travelling exhibition called 'Space Invaders' for the British Council. Softroom's interest in the creation of stimulating environments has also brought ongoing commissions for virtual sets for television, advertising campaigns and digital media.

Softroom sees itself as a practice that reacts to its clients. It was the first of its generation to adapt to the new-media environment via technology and communication. Softroom combines tradition and innovation, yet insists upon commercial pragmatism.

2

3

1

1|2 Office refurbishment,
Soho, London
3 Restaurant
refurbishment,
Finchley, London

4 Restaurant refurbishment, Soho, London

5|6 Shelter, Kielder Belvedere National Park, Northumbria

Stickland Coombe Architecture
258 Lavender Hill
London SW11 1LT
T   020 7924 1699
F   020 7652 1788
E   nick@scadesign.freeserve.co.uk

Stickland Coombe Architecture

Jonathan Stickland and Nick Coombe formed this practice in 1993 after meeting while working at Pierre d'Avoine. Their built work to date comprises domestic environments and art installations, but they are keen to gain opportunities in more total architectural inventions. They are committed to ecologically responsible design solutions, which affects the selection of products and materials and the choice of heating and ventilation techniques.

The winner of the FX Awards for Best Residence, their design for a duplex flat created the illusion of a larger space from a dark flat with cramped box-like spaces. They managed to bring light to the centre of the building by demolishing all the internal walls, creating one space. A tapered wall of back-lit polycarbonate sliding panels conceals a shelving system and the lighting tubes are sleeved according to the seasons: cool for the summer, warm for the winter.

The presentation of completed projects by Nick Coombe is thoughtful. Coombe has an intelligent and imaginative approach to the architectural process.

The practice seeks to generate bespoke solutions for projects, rather than sticking to a house style. Its projects demonstrate a commitment to working sensitively with clients and existing environments.

1 Residential refurbishment, Barbican, London
2 'Abracadabra', exhibition design, Tate Britain, Pimlico, London

3 Residential
  conversion, Chelsea,
  London
4 Residential
  conversion, South
  Kensington, London

Studio Downie
146 New Cavendish Street
London W1W 6YG
T 020 7255 1599
F 020 7636 7883
E studiodownie@studiodownie.com

Studio Downie

Studio Downie was established in 1992, when it was shortlisted in Europan. In 1993 it won the competition to design the sculpture gallery and visitors' pavilion on the Goodwood Estate, West Sussex. In the same year the practice was approved as consultant for the London Docklands Development Corporation and since then it has won a number of awards and been shortlisted for several prestigious projects.

In 1996 Craig Downie was appointed design advisor for the new second terminal at Heathrow Airport.

Clients have included the French Treasury, Microsoft/KMPG, the Institute of Contemporary Arts, The Image Bank and Corpus Christi College, Cambridge.

Simplicity, elegance and pragmatism are the key elements of Studio Downie's built forms. It was recently appointed as architect for the Royal Geographical Society and is to design the society's headquarters at Kensington Gore in west London, for completion in 2003.

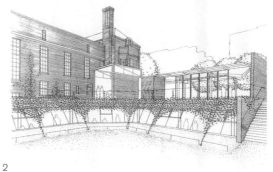

1

1 Next Step
Opportunities Centre,
Hayes, London
2 Gallery, Reading
Room and Archives,
Royal Geographical
Society, London

2

4 Office
refurbishment,
Hounslow,
London

3

4

Studio MG Architects
101 Turnmill Street
London EC1M 5QP
T   020 7251 2648
F   020 7490 8070
E   mail@studio

Studio MG Architects

Studio MG has worked with a range of clients providing solutions to briefs across the ecclesiastical, leisure, office and residential sectors. Its client list includes The Ivy Restaurant, Southwark and Hackney Councils, Acid Jazz Records, Fuji Films and Swiss Re-insurance. The practice is based in Clerkenwell, east London, but has established links with practices in Paris, Stuttgart and Beirut. It says its prime responsibility is to help its clients maximize the return on their investment in design and financial terms.

The practice has developed a collaborative approach to its clients and other professionals. Its teaching links provide a way of recharging ideas and challenging complacency.

Recent projects include a £1.5m restaurant in London, a £2.5m leisure centre in Oxford, a £4m arts centre in Peterborough and several private domestic developments.

1|2 Residential extension, Fulham Broadway, London

3 Yeung's bar and restaurant, London

3

4

4|5 Creche, new-build, Paris, France (collaboration with Atelier Kerosene)

5

Sutherland Hussey
3 Queen Charlotte Street
Edinburgh EH6 6BA
T 0131 553 4321
F 0131 554 6699
E charlies.architects@bigfoot.com

Sutherland Hussey

Charlie Sutherland and Charlie Hussey studied together at the Mackintosh School of Architecture, Glasgow, before both going on to work for Sir James Stirling on a number of internationally acclaimed buildings. In 1996 they set up their own practice in Edinburgh, combining running an office with part-time teaching at their alma mater. Although most of their work comes from London, they have projects stretching from Edinburgh to Truro in Cornwall. Their priority in all projects is to start by approaching each design problem with almost empirical objectivity. They hope that, through this rejection of preconceived ideas at the early stages of the design, new light will be shed on the creative potential of the program and the site.

The range of small projects they have completed so far is the result of intensive client-involvement in the design process, right from the early sketches. They find this to be not only essential in meeting the needs of the client, but also in making the process transparent. Their offices are based around a studio environment, which encourages practice members to explore one another's ideas. They very much enjoy the diversity of work they have so far undertaken and have no intention of moving into a specialist field, or indeed of growing into too big a practice; a move that they feel might obscure their ideals.

1 Emap Construction Tower, competition, 1997
2 Live/work, competition, Wood Green, London
3 Residential new-build, Barnhouse, Highgate, London

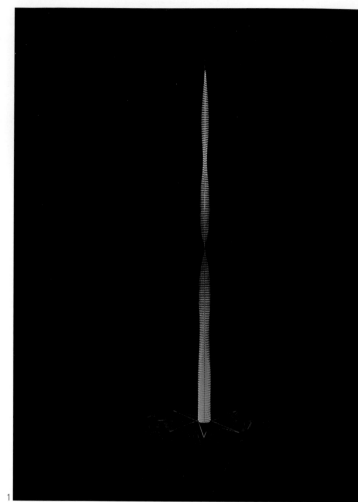

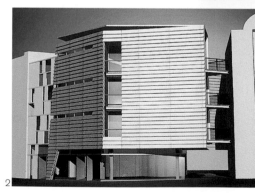

4

Tonkin Architects
24 Rosebery Avenue
London EC1
T 020 7837 6255
F 020 7837 6277
E tonkin@zoo.co.uk

Tonkin Architects

Set up by Mike Tonkin, the practice's portfolio includes residential, retail, office and restaurants, and it is complemented by competition work at the civic scale. Completed projects in Europe, East Asia and England have been published in books and periodicals, and have received several awards.

The practice's ethos is based on "asking, looking, playing, making", and its work aims to access the primal nature in people, which it describes as "the basic attraction to light, the need for patterns and the instinct for movement". It believes in doing what it has not done before and starts each project with a blank canvas.

Current projects include: a new house and studio for a jeweller and photographer, in north London; a penthouse in Bayswater, west London; and a warehouse gallery in Shoreditch, east London.

Tonkin Architects' approach is an unusual and innovative departure. It involves a readjustment of traditional priorities to create an architecture which is akin to light sculpture. Much emphasis is given to researching new materials and giving new use to traditional materials such as chipboard. The practice will make its mark very soon. Its house for a photographer and jeweller, in north London, reveals a lightness of touch in which a large pinhole camera becomes a studio and the storage areas become jewel-like pods. It demonstrates a close understanding of the lifestyle of the clients. The result is genuinely innovative in its concepts and method of execution.

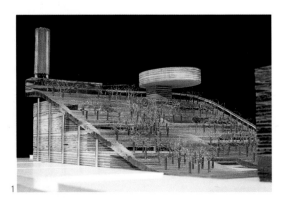

1 Tokyo Forum Competition, Tokyo, Japan
2 Residential new-build, Hong Kong, China
3 Residential new-build, Muswell Hill, London
4 Gallery conversion, 'One in the Other Gallery', Shoreditch, London

Urban Research Laboratory
3 Plantain Place
Crosby Row
London SE1 1YN
T   020 7403 2929
F   020 7403 0353
E   info@urbanresearchlab.com

Urban Research Laboratory

This practice was founded in 1997 on the idea that most architects had been disappointing developers for years. Its members felt that by understanding the market, the needs of its clients and the technical and commercial realities of building in a commercial marketplace, it could create better buildings and increase income for its clients. In an assessment of the London property and development business, Business magazine identified it as one of the most important companies of the next generation.

The practice is currently working on an urban regeneration scheme at a Dockland Light Railway station in Lewisham, south east London. The development comprises a 21-storey tower, a supermarket, many low-rise flats, commercial spaces, cafes, restaurants and an art gallery.

An unconventional practice, with a charismatic figurehead in Jeff Kirby. The development of Urban Research Laboratory is exciting to watch. It is a relief to encounter a practice that is not afraid of looking at the bigger picture. Kirby's property developer 'nous' has influenced his clients to incorporate environmental aspects into their schemes and to make the 'urban gesture' that is the practice's primary concern.

The practice takes its cue from the work of the Government's Urban Task Force initiative which seeks to create a national urban design framework, and sees itself as having a responsibility in this area.

The practice's concerns transcend the conventional conception of an architect's role and it is this that really sets URL apart. It is inspiring to see a young practice being bold, 'blowing-the-trumpet' for architecture, and positioning a new role for architectural practice.

2

1 Visualizations for 'The Pod', realized residential spaces in Bermondsey, London
2 Residential refurbishment and conversion, Barnes, London

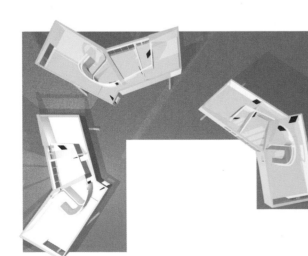

1

3 Residential
conversion,
Islington, London
4|5 Residential
conversion, 'The Pod'
Bermondsey,
London

Urban Salon
Unit D
Flat Iron Yard
Ayres Street
London SE1 1ES
T 020 7357 8300
F 020 7407 2800
E urbansalonltd@btinternet.com

Urban Salon

Urban Salon was established in 1995 as a vehicle for the exploration of both live and theoretical urban, architectural and design projects. One of its aims is to bring an increased ecological bias to its projects, and to address such issues as energy consumption and the sources of building materials. The work covers a range of exhibitions, events, domestic and commercial buildings and interiors.

Clients include the RIBA, the ICA, The New Millennium Experience Company and Mother. Recent projects include the design of a floating house on the River Thames and a house of the future for Orange Communications. The latter incorporated pioneering communications and automated systems by Orange which would be suitable for a typical family. The technology was completely integrated into the house so that inhabitants could feel the benefits but not be overwhelmed. The house, now completed, will act as a research centre and test-bed for future technologies. Families, focus groups and educational groups will be invited to visit or live in the house as part of Orange's ongoing research program. The project was covered widely in the national and trade press.

Urban Salon has a diverse body of work that differs from the usual collection of house extensions that one sees from most young practices. Its interest in temporary architecture led to the Skyscape project next to the Millennium Dome, which is by far its most substantial project and is interesting in the way that it has adopted technology more usually used in sets for rock concerts. It is on a unique site and performs particular function successfully.

Much of the rest of the practice's high-profile work has been in exhibition design, including the work at the ICA, Crafts Council and the Rem Koolhaas exhibition at the RIBA. This is very good work and has clearly helped the practice to form its ideas on the possibilities for temporary locations.

Urban Salon is interesting in that its practice is not founded on an aesthetic or stylistic premise. It has a clear agenda: to form multi-disciplinary teams tackling projects on the margins of conventional building and architecture. The practice is not easy to categorize, but seems to have found a rich seam of its own to mine.

1

2

1|2 Residential prototype, Orange @ Home, Orange Communications, Hatfield

3 Reception, Cearns and Brown Ltd, Runcorn, Cheshire

4|5 Exhibition design, Portable Architecture Exhibition, RIBA, London

Ushida Findlay Office
94 Leonard Street
London EC2A 4RH
T   020 7613 4972
F   020 7613 5849
E   ushifind@globalnet.co.uk

Ushida Findlay Office

This practice was established in London in 1998, and has grown steadily over the last three years. It is a design-driven practice, seeking to create original buildings developed from a close relationship with the client and an understanding of context and technology.

UF has worked with a variety of clients on different scales, from a £10,000 arts project to a £3.5m sports proposal. Currently, the practice is building a range of domestic projects in London and completing a 6,000 sq m office fit-out, which includes bespoke furniture, for an advertising agency. It has recently been shortlisted in a number of design competitions, including those for Lichfield Cultural Quarter in Hampshire, Pier Arts Centre in Orkney and Tinside Lido in Plymouth.

UF seeks to exploit traditional and advanced technologies to generate specific solutions that challenge preconceived notions of architecture while still producing realistic and deliverable buildings.

Ushida Findlay's work is innovative and recognizable, despite the architect's denial of a house style. The work does show a distinct regard for 'craft' in buildings, a delight in materials such as bamboo and thatch as well as a penchant for curves. Reason and logic lie behind all the choices. The work displays a discernible Japanese influence, and an appreciation of landscape and lighting. In short, intelligent, well-honed projects in a small portfolio.

2

3

1

1|4 The Pool House, South East England
2 Residential refurbishment, Southwark, London
3 Office refurbishment, Battersea, London

Walker and Martin
Morelands Building
9–15 Old Street
London EC1V 9HL
T   020 7253 8624
F   020 7253 8625
E   wam@walkerandmartin.co.uk

Walker and Martin

This practice started in 1995 without a complex agenda and with an attitude that it describes as "laid-back". This continues today, it says, even though the practice is handling projects worth up to £5m for blue-chip clients. It says a key part of its approach is "pushing clients to 'think out of the box', resulting in exciting concepts and successful projects that have been described as having the 'W&M Factor'". The client list includes Thomas Cook, Allgood, Aram Designs and Avis.

The practice considers itself a specialist in call-centre design and David Walker was part of the Estates Gazette discussion on the topic in 1998. It enjoys collaborative projects and has worked with furniture designer Alison Borer, public artists Jonathan Cassells and Claire Taylor and carpet designers Milliken. Production will soon be starting on a series of door handles.

The practice's work to date has mainly been interiors. Schemes are colourful and playful, often using 'wit' and style to give clients fresh takes on their environments. The firm prides itself on a rational, thoughtful approach and a simple explanation of orientation. Work is to a tight budget but the practice maximises that limitation through innovative features. W&M are now just breaking into new-build work, with a headquarters project proposed for Ashford, Kent. In summary, the firm's approach is bold, fun and unusual, but accomplished.

1|2 Thomas Cook
    Worldwide,
    headquarters,
    London
3|4 Thomas Cook
    Group, call centre,
    Peterborough

Wilkinson King Architects
Unit 6 Burghley Yard
106 Burghley Road
London NW3 1AL
T   020 7284 1975
F   020 7284 1984
E   architects@wilkinsonking.com

Wilkinson King Architects

Julian King and Chantal Wilkinson formed this practice in 1995. King worked for a number of years at Nicholas Grimshaw and Partners, where he worked on a number of projects, including Pier 4A at Heathrow Airport and the RAC command and control centre in Bristol. Wilkinson studied interior design before she moved into architectural studies at the Royal College of Art, and has since worked with architects such as Harper Mackay. Together they have won a number of important competitions including Europan 4, for the Castle Vale Estate in Birmingham. The project dealt with the regeneration of an existing housing estate using a programme of careful intervention with landscaping and new-building. The scheme also explored the relationship of the estate to its surrounding environment and community.

The practice is currently working on a range of projects that includes a swimming-pool facility for special-needs children at Haymerle School in Peckham, south London, a retail and workshop development on Hatton Garden in central London and a call centre for Cap Gemini in Bristol.

This practice wants to remain broad-based and learn from the cross-section of projects it has completed to date, so as to employ an open-minded and professional approach to all current and future projects.

1

3

1 Play Resource Centre, Staines, Surrey
2 Residential extension, Maida Vale, London
3|4 Residential extension, Wimbledon, London

Useful information

The Royal Institute of British Architects' Clients Advisory Service

The RIBA Clients Advisory Service (CAS) exists to assist clients in their selection of architects, initially by providing free lists of suitable practices according to the information provided by the client on their potential project. The information comes from an extensive database of all RIBA registered practices throughout the UK.

This unique service is available to anyone contemplating any building project and is designed to cater for both experienced clients and those who are building for the first time.

The information held on each practice includes:
● a practice profile
● sectors within which the practice has worked
● the range of services offered by the practice

The service operates from the RIBA headquarters in London:
Clients Advisory Service
Royal Institute of British Architects
66 Portland Place
London W1N 4AD
T 020 7307 3700
F 020 7436 9112
E cas@inst.riba.org
W www.architecture.com

The Royal Incorporation of Architects in Scotland (RIAS)
should also be contacted for information on any Scottish practices:
Royal Incorporation of Architects in Scotland
15 Rutland Square
Edinburgh
EH1 2BE
T 0131 229 7205
F 0131 228 2188
E info@rias.org.uk
W www.rias.org.uk

National Architecture Centre Network
The aim of the National Architecture Centre Network is to promote, maintain and advance education, public participation and design excellence in architecture, urban design and other design disciplines relating to the built environment through exhibitions, events and design initiatives.

CUBE (Centre for Understanding the Built Environment)
117 Portland Street
Manchester M1 6FB
T 0161 237 5525
F 0161 236 5815
E info@cubeuk.org
W www.cubeuk.org

Hackney Building Exploratory
Professional Development Centre
Albion Drive
London E8 4ET
T 020 7275 8555
F 020 7275 8555
E nicole@buildingexploratory.org.uk

LADT (Liverpool Architecture and Design Trust)
16 Vernon Street
Liverpool L2
T 0151 233 4079
F 0151 233 4078
E tonywoolf@mailandrews.com

London Open House
Unit C1
Linton House
39/51 Highgate Road
London NW5 1RS
T 020 7267 7644
F 020 7267 2822
E gen@londonopenhouse.org
W www.architecturelink.org.uk

Northern Architecture
Blackfriars
Monk Street
Newcastle upon Tyne
NE1 4XN
T 0191 260 2191
F 0191 260 2191
E na@north.org.uk
W www.north.org.uk

RIBA Architecture Gallery
66 Portland Place
London W1N 4AD
T 020 7307 3699
F 020 7307 3703
E noel.bramley@inst.riba.org

Plymouth Architectural Trust
C/o Hillside House
Browston Street
Modbury
Devon PL21
T 01548 830 850
F 01548 830 342
E adriangale@uku.co.uk

The Architecture Centre
Narrow Quay
Bristol BS1 4QA
T 0117 922 1540
F 0117 922 1541
E m.pearson@ukgateway.net

The Architecture Foundation
60 Bastwick Street
London EC1V 3TN
T 020 7253 3334
F 020 7253 3335
E mail@architecturefoundation.org.uk
W www.architecturefoundation.org.uk

The Kent Architecture Centre
Chatham Historic Dockyard
Kent ME4 4TE
T 01634 401 166
F 01634 403 302
E info@kentarchitecture.co.uk
W www.kentarchitecture.co.uk

The Lighthouse
56 Mitchell Street
Glasgow G1 3LX
T 0141 221 6362
F 0141 221 6395
W www.lighthouse.co.uk

Concourse
34 College Grove Road
Wakefield WF1 3RE
T 01924 374 293
F 01924 374 293
E graham.roberts@btinternet.com

MADE (Midlands Architecture Design Environment)
RIBA West Midlands Region
Birmingham and Midlands Institute
Margaret Street
Birmingham B3 3SP
T 0121 233 2321
F 0121 233 4946
E julia.ellis@member.riba.org

Information about the National Architecture Centre Network can be found at www.architecturecentre.net, which has direct links to all the centres above.

Acknowledgements

The Architecture Foundation would like to thank the following sponsors, organisations and individuals who have generously contributed to the success of this project

CABE
Delancey Estates plc
with support from
The British Council

Wordsearch
Rebecca Lesser
Lee Mallett
Peter Murray
Sophie Murray
Hannah Weir

Jury
Amanda Baillieu, Editor, Riba Journal, London
Nigel Coates, Branson Coates Architects, London
Tania Concko, Tania Concko Architects, Amsterdam
Terence Conran, Director, Conran and Partners, London
Paul Finch, CABE Commissioner, London
Tony Hunt, Anthony Hunt & Associates, Cirencester (Chair)
Louisa Hutton, Sauerbruch Hutton Architects, Berlin
Professor Isi Metzstein, Glasgow
James Ritblat, Chairman, Delancey Estates, London

Assessors
Professor Peter Fawcett
Sarah Featherstone
Robert Firth
Adrian Gale
Alastair Hall
Tom Jefferies
Helen Jones
Matthew Lloyd
Colen Lumley
Kieran Long
Michael Manser
Dr Stuart McDonald
Professor Charles McKean
Robert Mull
Marko Piplica
Professor Wendy Potts
Jack Pringle
David Taylor
Sniez Torbarina
Terry Trickett
Santa Raymond
Kester Rattenbury
David Rosen
Nigel Woolner

The Architecture Foundation
Trustees:
Richard Rogers (Founding Chair)
Will Alsop (Chair)
Garry Hart (Deputy Chair)
Richard Burdett
Nigel Coates
Dr Francis Duffy
David Gordon
Zaha Hadid
Professor Sir Peter Hall
Derek Higgs
Nigel Hugill
Simon Jenkins
Amanda Levete
Alan Yentob

Director: Lucy Musgrave
Deputy Director: Haruo Morishima
Publications Co-ordinator: Hannah Ford
Project Assistant: Eve Chung
Press Co-ordinator: Tamzyn Emery

Special thanks to Julia Read, Bridget Sawyers, Simon Esterson, Jon Hill, Hannah Tyson, Matthew Brown, James Ritblat, Jane Galilee, Paul Zara and all the architects involved

The Architecture Foundation is largely reliant on the generosity of the private sector, not only to enable our projects but to stabilise the organisation. We are extremely grateful to the following for their vital support towards our core funding: CABE (Commission for Architecture and the Built Environment), The Esmée Fairbairn Charitable Trust, The Glass-House Trust, Capital & Provident Regeneration Ltd, The Wates Foundation, Ove Arup Partnership, John Lewis Partnership, British Land, Laing's Charitable Trust, Bovis Construction, Berkeley Homes, Manhattan Loft Corporation Ltd, Hammerson plc, Sloane Robinson Investment Management Ltd, Jones Lang LaSalle

We would like to thank the Patrons of the Architecture Foundation Membership Scheme whose subscriptions contribute towards the organisation's stability: Adams Kara Taylor, Allies and Morrison, Lorraine Baldry, Broadway Malyan, C2 Architects, The Crown Estate, Edward Cullinan Architects, Entech Environmental Technology Ltd, EPR Architects, Max Fordham, Feilden Clegg Bradley Architects, Fulcrum Consulting, Gensler , David Goldstein , GMW Partnership, Kohn Pedersen Fox International, Lifschutz Davidson Ltd, McDowell + Benedetti,

Chiji Okeke, ORMS Designers & Architects Ltd, Phaidon Press Ltd, Sudhu Prabhu, Price & Myers, Roberts & Partners Ltd, Slough Estates plc, Geoffrey Wilson

We are also grateful for in-kind core support from: Access Storage, Ahrend, The Economist, Erco, Herbert Smith, Lomas Davies, Metro New Media, Robin Day/Hille International, Tapestry, V.I.P Very Interesting Paper Co Ltd, Wildgoose

Images appear by kind permission of the following (page number followed by image number): p13 (1, 2) Lyndon Douglas; p21 (2) Chris Morris, (3) Nicholas Kane; p24-25 (1|2, 3|4) Sue Barr; p26-27 (2, 3) David Grandorge; p28-29 (1|2) James Morris, (3) Eamonn O'Mahoney, (4|5) Paul Harmer; p30-31 (1|2) Valerie Bennett, (3|4) Megha Chand; p32-33 (1-5) Alan Williams; p34 (2) Todd Watson, (3) Errol Forbes; p36-37 (1-4) Marianne Majerus; p40-41 (2-5) Photec; p42 (1-5) Nick Kane; p44-45 (1) Kenan Klico, (2-5) Paul Tyagi; p48 (2) Martin Peters; p50-51 (1, 4|5) Richard Glover Photography; p52-53 (2) Sue Barr, (3) Hélène Binet; p54-55 (1-3) Michael Morans; p59 (3|4) Martin Charles; p60-61 (1|2) Sinisa Savic, (3|4) Mike Redfern; p62-63 (1|2) Richard Davies, (3|4) Rod Coyne; p64 (1) Tony Wilkonson, (2) Tom Mannion; p66-67 (1-3) Nick Kane; p68 (1, 2) Nick Kane; p70-71 (1|2, 3) Polly Farquharson; p74-75 (1) Martine Hamilton-Knight, (2) Creative Circle, (3) David Grandorge; p78-79 (1, 3|4) Chris Gascoigne/View, (2) Andrew Putler; p80-81 (1|2) Martine Hamilton-Knight, (3, 4) Bob Berry; p82-83 (1) Charlotte Wood, (2) Jonathan Moore, (3|4) Neil Armitage; p84-85 (1, 3|4) David Churchill; p86-87 (1, 3|4) David Stewart; p88 (1, 2) Derek Santini; p90-91(1) Paul Tyagi (2-4) Gary Taylor; p92-93 (1, 3-6) David Grandorge, (2) Sue Barr; p94-95 (1-4) James Morris; p96-97 (2) Ronald Yee, (4) Clive Frost; p100-101 (1-5) Martine Hamilton-Knight; p102-103 (1|5) Jennifer Hands, (2) Jane Kattein, (3) Jacques Russell Ltd; p104-105 (1-4) Martin McCabe; p106-107 (1) Nick Wood, (2, 3) Morley Von Sternberg; p108-109 (1-4) Peter Cook/View; p110-111 (1-4) Dennis Gilbert/View; p112-113 (1, 3, 4) Andrew Lee; p116-117 (2, 4) Dan Weldon; p118-119 (1-4) Simon Doling; p120-121 (2|4) Holger Rehne, (3) Peter Gunzel; p122-123 (4) Sue Barr; p126-127 (1) Christain Aschman, (2|3) Hélène Binet, (4) David Grandorge; p128-129 (1) Sue Barr, (4|5) Julian Cornish-Trestrail; p130 (1) Johannes Schwartz; p132-133 (2, 3, 4) Paul Smoothy; p134-135 (2) Mattias Ek (4, 5) David Grandorge; p136-137 (1, 3, 4) David Churchill, (2) James Morris; p138-139 (1|2) Max Alexander, (3, 4) Richard Glover, (5|6) Keith Paisley; p140-141 (1|2, 3) Paul Tyagi; p146-147 (2) Andrew Wood; p150-151 (1|2, 4|5) Phil Sayer; p152-153 (1|4) James Harris; p154-155 (1|2) Peter Durant/Arcblue, (3|4) Morley von Sternberg; p156-157 (1-4) Paul Tyagi.

Every effort has been made to acknowledge correctly and contact the source and copyright holder of each picture. The publisher apologises for any unintentional errors or omissions.

The British Council has contributed energetically to the promotion of British architecture overseas during the past five years, and our commitment to architecture as an expression of the creativity and critical dynamism of the UK is growing.

British architects are patronized through commissions for British Council properties abroad – including, recently, Sauerbruch Hutton in Berlin, Germany, and Casson Mann in Thessaloniki, Greece – and for the design of our international touring exhibitions of British design – recent examples include the design of *Inside Out: Underwear and Style in the UK* by Branson Coates, *Lost & Found* by muf, *Home Sweet Home* by Softroom, and most recently, *Space Invaders* by Urban Salon.

Space Invaders celebrates before an international audience the distinctive, cross-disciplinary, socially integrated approach of many of Britain's younger architectural practices. The exhibition invites 15 practices, a majority of which appear in *New Architects 2*, to demonstrate the way in which they extend the concept of architecture beyond the design of buildings through four thematic ideas: the influence of 'everyday' or popular culture, the talking, legible city, border cultures and visions of the future. Curated by Lucy Bullivant and Pedro Gadhano, with the British Council, *Space Invaders* opens concurrently with the launch of this book, in Portugal at the Lisbon design biennial, 'Experimenta 2001', and is an invaluable support of the British Council's argument in the exhibition and in its larger program.

Emily Campbell
Art, Architecture & Design
The British Council

The British Council